JAMESTOWN EDUCATION

Timed Readings Plus *in Science*

25 Two-Part Lessons
with Questions for
Building Reading Speed and Comprehension

BOOK 4

Glencoe
McGraw-Hill

New York, New York   Columbus, Ohio   Chicago, Illinois   Peoria, Illinois   Woodland Hills, California

JAMESTOWN EDUCATION

Glencoe/McGraw-Hill

A Division of The McGraw·Hill Companies

ISBN: 0-07-827373-0

Send all queries to:
Glencoe/McGraw-Hill
8787 Orion Place
Columbus, OH 43240-4027

1 2 3 4 5 6 7 8 9 10 021 08 07 06 05 04 03 02

CONTENTS

TO THE STUDENT

You probably talk at an average rate of about 150 words a minute. If you are a reader of average ability, you read at a rate of about 250 words a minute. So your reading speed is nearly twice as fast as your speaking or listening speed. This example shows that reading is one of the fastest ways to get information.

The purpose of this book is to help you increase your reading rate and understand what you read. The 25 lessons in this book will also give you practice in reading science articles and in preparing for tests in which you must read and understand nonfiction passages within a certain time limit.

Reading Faster and Better

Following are some strategies that you can use to read the articles in each lesson.

Previewing

Previewing before you read is a very important step. This helps you to get an idea of what a selection is about and to recall any previous knowledge you have about the subject. Here are the steps to follow when previewing.

Read the title. Titles are designed not only to announce the subject but also to make the reader think. Ask yourself questions such as What can I learn from the title? What thoughts does it bring to mind?

What do I already know about this subject?

Read the first sentence. If they are short, read the first two sentences. The opening sentence is the writer's opportunity to get your attention. Some writers announce what they hope to tell you in the selection. Some writers state their purpose for writing; others just try to get your attention.

Read the last sentence. If it is short, read the final two sentences. The closing sentence is the writer's last chance to get ideas across to you. Some writers repeat the main idea once more. Some writers draw a conclusion—this is what they have been leading up to. Other writers summarize their thoughts; they tie all the facts together.

Skim the entire selection. Glance through the selection quickly to see what other information you can pick up. Look for anything that will help you read fluently and with understanding. Are there names, dates, or numbers? If so, you may have to read more slowly.

Reading for Meaning

Here are some ways to make sure you are making sense of what you read.

Build your concentration. You cannot understand what you read if you are not concentrating. When you discover that your thoughts are straying, correct the situation right away. Avoid distractions and distracting situations. Keep in mind the information you learned from previewing. This will help focus your attention on the selection.

Read in thought groups. Try to see meaningful combinations of words—phrases, clauses, or sentences. If you look at only one word at a time (called word-by-word reading), both your comprehension and your reading speed suffer.

Ask yourself questions. To sustain the pace you have set for yourself and to maintain a high level of concentration and comprehension, ask yourself questions such as What does this mean? or How can I use this information? as you read.

Finding the Main Ideas

The paragraph is the basic unit of meaning. If you can quickly discover and understand the main idea of each paragraph, you will build your comprehension of the selection.

Find the topic sentence. The topic sentence, which contains the main idea, often is the first sentence of a paragraph. It is followed by sentences that support, develop, or explain the main idea. Sometimes a topic sentence comes at the end of a paragraph. When it does, the supporting details come first, building the base for the topic sentence. Some paragraphs do not have a topic sentence; all of the sentences combine to create a meaningful idea.

Understand paragraph structure. Every well-written paragraph has a purpose. The purpose may be to inform, define, explain or illustrate. The purpose should always relate to the main idea and expand on it. As you read each paragraph, see how the body of the paragraph tells you more about the main idea.

Relate ideas as you read. As you read the selection, notice how the writer puts together ideas. As you discover the relationship between the ideas, the main ideas come through quickly and clearly.

Mastering Reading Comprehension

Reading fast is not useful if you don't remember or understand what you read. The two exercises in Part A provide a check on how well you have understood the article.

Recalling Facts

These multiple-choice questions provide a quick check to see how well you recall important information from the article. As you learn to apply the reading strategies described earlier, you should be able to answer these questions more successfully.

Understanding Ideas

These questions require you to think about the main ideas in the article. Some main ideas are stated in the article; others are not. To answer some of the questions, you need to draw conclusions about what you read.

The five exercises in Part B require multiple answers. These exercises provide practice in applying comprehension and critical thinking skills that you can use in all your reading.

Recognizing Words in Context

Always check to see whether the words around an unfamiliar word—its context—can give you a clue to the word's meaning. A word generally appears in a context related to its meaning.

Suppose, for example, that you are unsure of the meaning of the word *expired* in the following passage:

> Vera wanted to check out a book, but her library card had expired. She had to borrow my card, because she didn't have time to renew hers.

You could begin to figure out the meaning of *expired* by asking yourself a question such as, What could have happened to Vera's library card that would make her need to borrow someone else's card? You might realize that if Vera had to renew her card, its usefulness must have come to an end or run out. This would lead you to conclude that the word *expired* must mean "to come to an end" or "to run out." You would be right. The context suggested the meaning.

Context can also affect the meaning of a word you already know. The word *key*, for instance, has many meanings. There are musical keys, door keys, and keys to solving a mystery. The context in which the word *key* occurs will tell you which meaning is correct.

Sometimes a word is explained by the words that immediately follow it. The subject of a sentence and your knowledge about that subject might also help you determine the meaning of an unknown word. Try to decide the meaning of the word *revive* in the following sentence:

> Sunshine and water will revive those drooping plants.

The compound subject is *sunshine* and *water*. You know that plants need light and water to survive and that drooping plants are not healthy. You can figure out that *revive* means "to bring back to health."

Distinguishing Fact from Opinion

Every day you are called upon to sort out fact and opinion. Because much of what you read and hear contains both facts and opinions, you need to be able to tell the two apart.

Facts are statements that can be proved true. The proof must be objective and verifiable. You must be able to check for yourself to confirm a fact.

Look at the following facts. Notice that they can be checked for accuracy and confirmed. Suggested sources for verification appear in parentheses.

- Abraham Lincoln was the 16th president of the United States. (Consult biographies, social studies books, encyclopedias, and similar sources.)

- Earth revolves around the Sun. (Research in encyclopedias or astronomy books; ask knowledgeable people.)

- Dogs walk on four legs. (See for yourself.)

Opinions are statements that cannot be proved true. There is no objective evidence you can consult to check the truthfulness of an opinion. Unlike facts, opinions express personal beliefs or judgments. Opinions reveal how someone feels about a subject, not the facts about that subject. You might agree or disagree with someone's opinion, but you cannot prove it right or wrong.

Look at the following opinions. The reasons these statements are classified as opinions appear in parentheses.

- Abraham Lincoln was born to be a president. (You cannot prove this by referring to birth records. There is no evidence to support this belief.)

- Earth is the only planet in our solar system where intelligent life exists. (There is no proof of this. It may be proved true some day, but for now it is just an educated guess—not a fact.)

- The dog is a human's best friend. (This is not a fact; your best friend might not be a dog.)

As you read, be aware that facts and opinions are often mixed together. Both are useful to you as a reader. But to evaluate what you read and to read intelligently, you need to know the difference between the two.

Keeping Events in Order

Sequence, or chronological order, is the order of events in a story or article or the order of steps in a process. Paying attention to the sequence of events or steps will help you follow what is happening, predict what might happen next, and make sense of a passage.

To make the sequence as clear as possible, writers often use signal words to help the reader get a more exact idea of when things happen. Following is a list of frequently used signal words and phrases:

until	first
next	then
before	after
finally	later
when	while
during	now
at the end	by the time
as soon as	in the beginning

Signal words and phrases are also useful when a writer chooses to relate details or events out of sequence. You need to pay careful attention to determine the correct chronological order.

Making Correct Inferences

Much of what you read *suggests* more than it *says*. Writers often do not state ideas directly in a text. They can't. Think of the time and space it would take to state every idea. And think of how boring that would be! Instead, writers leave it to you, the reader, to fill in the information they leave out—to make inferences. You do this by combining clues in the story or article with knowledge from your own experience.

You make many inferences every day. Suppose, for example, that you are visiting a friend's house for the first time. You see a bag of kitty litter. You infer (make an inference) that the family has a cat. Another day you overhear a conversation. You catch the names of two actors and the words *scene, dialogue,* and *directing.* You infer that the people are discussing a movie or play.

In these situations and others like them, you infer unstated information from what you observe or read. Readers must make inferences in order to understand text.

Be careful about the inferences you make. One set of facts may suggest several inferences. Some of these inferences could be faulty. A correct inference must be supported by evidence.

Remember that bag of kitty litter that caused you to infer that your friend has a cat? That could be a faulty inference. Perhaps your friend's family uses the kitty litter on their icy sidewalks to create traction. To be sure your inference is correct, you need more evidence.

Understanding Main Ideas

The main idea is the most important idea in a paragraph or passage—the idea that provides purpose and direction. The rest of the selection explains, develops, or supports the main idea. Without a main idea, there would be only a collection of unconnected thoughts.

In the following paragraph, the main idea is printed in italics. As you read, observe how the other sentences develop or explain the main idea.

Typhoon Chris hit with full fury today on the central coast of Japan. Heavy rain from the storm flooded the area. High waves carried many homes into the sea. People now fear that the heavy rains will cause mudslides in the central part of the country. The number of people killed by the storm may climb past the 200 mark by Saturday.

In this paragraph, the main-idea statement appears first. It is followed by sentences that explain, support, or give details. Sometimes the main idea appears at the end of a paragraph. Writers often put the main idea at the end of a paragraph when their purpose is to persuade or convince. Readers may be more open to a new idea if the reasons for it are presented first.

As you read the following paragraph, think about the overall impact of the supporting ideas. Their purpose is to convince the reader that the main idea in the last sentence should be accepted.

Last week there was a head-on collision at Huntington and Canton streets. Just a month ago a pedestrian was struck there. Fortunately, she was only slightly injured. In the past year, there have been more accidents there than at any other corner in the city. In fact, nearly 10 percent of all accidents in the city occur at the corner. This intersection is very dangerous, and a traffic signal should be installed there before a life is lost.

The details in the paragraph progress from least important to most important. They achieve their full effect in the main idea statement at the end.

In many cases, the main idea is not expressed in a single sentence. The reader is called upon to interpret all of the ideas expressed in the paragraph and to decide upon a main idea. Read the following paragraph.

The American author Jack London was once a pupil at the Cole Grammar School in Oakland, California. Each morning the class sang a song. When the teacher noticed that Jack wouldn't sing, she sent him to the principal. He returned to class with a note. The note said that Jack could be excused from singing with the class if he would write an essay every morning.

In this paragraph, the reader has to interpret the individual ideas and to decide on a main idea. This main idea seems reasonable: Jack London's career as a writer began with a punishment in grammar school.

Understanding the concept of the main idea and knowing how to find it is important. Transferring that understanding to your reading and study is also important.

Working Through a Lesson

Part A

1. **Preview the article.** Locate the timed selection in Part A of the lesson that you are going to read. Wait for your teacher's signal to preview. You will have 20 seconds for previewing. Follow the previewing steps described on page 2.

2. **Read the article.** When your teacher gives you the signal, begin reading. Read carefully so that you will be able to answer questions about what you have read. When you finish reading, look at the board and note your reading time. Write this time at the bottom of the page on the line labeled Reading Time.

3. **Complete the exercises.** Answer the 10 questions that follow the article. There are 5 fact questions and 5 idea questions. Choose the best answer to each question and put an X in that box.

4. **Correct your work.** Use the Answer Key at the back of the book to check your answers. Circle any wrong answer and put an X in the box you should have marked. Record the number of correct answers on the appropriate line at the end of the lesson.

Part B

1. **Preview and read the passage.** Use the same techniques you

used to read Part A. Think about what you are reading.

2. **Complete the exercises.** Instructions are given for answering each category of question. There are 15 responses for you to record.

3. **Correct your work.** Use the Answer Key at the back of the book. Circle any wrong answer and write the correct letter or number next to it. Record the number of correct answers on the appropriate line at the end of the lesson.

Plotting Your Progress

1. **Find your reading rate.** Turn to the Reading Rate graph on page 116. Put an X at the point where the vertical line that represents the lesson intersects your reading time, shown along the left-hand side. The right-hand side of the graph will reveal your words-per-minute reading speed.

2. **Find your comprehension score.** Add your scores for Part A and Part B to determine your total number of correct answers. Turn to the Comprehension Score Graph on page 117. Put an X at the point where the vertical line that represents your lesson intersects your total correct answers, shown along the left-hand side. The right-hand side of the graph will show the percentage of questions you answered correctly.

3. **Complete the Comprehension Skills Profile.** Turn to page 118. Record your incorrect answers for the Part B exercises. The five Part B skills are listed along the bottom. There are five columns of boxes, one column for each question. For every incorrect answer, put an X in a box for that skill.

To get the most benefit from these lessons, you need to take charge of your own progress in improving your reading speed and comprehension. Studying these graphs will help you to see whether your reading rate is increasing and to determine what skills you need to work on. Your teacher will also review the graphs to check your progress.

TO THE TEACHER

About the Series

Timed Readings Plus in Science includes 10 books at reading levels 4–13, with one book at each level. Book One contains material at a fourth-grade reading level; Book Two at a fifth-grade level, and so on. The readability level is determined by the Fry Readability Scale and is not to be confused with grade or age level. The books are designed for use with students at middle school level and above.

The purposes of the series are as follows:

- to provide systematic, structured reading practice that helps students improve their reading rate and comprehension skills

- to give students practice in reading and understanding informational articles in the content area of science

- to give students experience in reading various text types—informational, expository, narrative, and prescriptive

- to prepare students for taking standardized tests that include timed reading passages in various content areas

- to provide materials with a wide range of reading levels so that students can continue to practice and improve their reading rate and comprehension skills

Because the books are designed for use with students at designated reading levels rather than in a particular grade, the science topics in this series are not correlated to any grade-level curriculum. Most standardized tests require students to read and comprehend science passages. This series provides an opportunity for students to become familiar with the particular requirements of reading science. For example, the vocabulary in a science article is important. Students need to know certain words in order to understand the concepts and the information.

Each book in the series contains 25 two-part lessons. Part A focuses on improving reading rate. This section of the lesson consists of a 400-word timed informational article on a science topic followed by two multiple-choice exercises. Recalling Facts includes five fact questions; Understanding Ideas includes five critical-thinking questions.

Part B concentrates on building mastery in critical areas of comprehension. This section consists of a nontimed passage—the "plus" passage—followed by five exercises that address five major comprehension skills. The passage varies in length; its subject matter relates to the content of the timed selection.

Timed Reading and Comprehension

Timed reading is the best-known method of improving reading speed. There is no point in someone's reading at an accelerated speed if the person does not understand what she or he is reading. Nothing is more important than comprehension in reading. The main purpose of reading is to gain knowledge and insight, to understand the information that the writer and the text are communicating.

Few students will be able to read a passage once and answer all of the questions correctly. A score of 70 or 80 percent correct is normal. If the student gets 90 or 100 percent correct, he or she is either reading too slowly or the material is at too low a reading level. A comprehension or critical thinking score of less than 70 percent indicates a need for improvement.

One method of improving comprehension and critical thinking skills is for the student to go back and study each incorrect answer. First, the student should reread the question carefully. It is surprising how many students get the wrong answer simply because they have not read the question carefully. Then the student should look back in the passage to find the place where the question is answered, reread that part of the passage, and think about how to arrive at the correct answer. It is important to be able to recognize a correct answer when it is embedded in the text. Teacher guidance or class discussion will help the student find an answer.

Speed Versus Comprehension

It is not unusual for comprehension scores to decline as reading rate increases during the early weeks of timed readings. If this happens, students should attempt to level off their speed—but not lower it—and concentrate more on comprehension. Usually, if students maintain the higher speed and concentrate on comprehension, scores will gradually improve and within a week or two be back up to normal levels of 70 to 80 percent.

It is important to achieve a proper balance between speed and comprehension. An inefficient reader typically reads everything at one speed, usually slowly. Some poor readers, however, read rapidly but without satisfactory comprehension. It is important to achieve a balance between speed and comprehension. The practice that this series provides enables students to increase their reading speed while maintaining normal levels of comprehension.

Getting Started

As a rule, the passages in a book designed to improve reading speed should be relatively easy. The student should not have much difficulty with the vocabulary or the subject matter. Don't worry about the passages being too easy; students should see how quickly and efficiently they can read a passage.

Begin by assigning students to a level. A student should start with a book that is one level below his or her current reading level. If a student's reading level is not known, a suitable starting point would be one or two levels below the student's present grade in school.

Introduce students to the contents and format of the book they are using. Examine the book to see how it is organized. Talk about the parts of each lesson. Discuss the purpose of timed reading and the use of the progress graphs at the back of the book.

Timing the Reading

One suggestion for timing the reading is to have all students begin reading the selection at the same time. After one minute, write on the board the time that has elapsed and begin updating it at 10-second intervals (1:00, 1:10, 1:20, etc.). Another option is to have individual students time themselves with a stopwatch.

Teaching a Lesson

Part A

1. Give students the signal to begin previewing the lesson. Allow 20 seconds, then discuss special science terms or vocabulary that students found.

2. Use one of the methods described above to time students as they read the passage, (Include the 20-second preview time as part of the first minute.) Tell students to write down the last time shown on the board or the stopwatch when they finish reading. Have them record the time in the designated space after the passage.

3. Next, have students complete the exercises in Part A. Work with them to check their answers, using the Answer Key that begins on page 114. Have them circle incorrect answers, mark the correct answers, and then record the numbers of correct answers for Part A on the appropriate line at the end of the lesson. Correct responses to eight or more questions indicate satisfactory comprehension and recall.

Part B

1. Have students read the Part B passage and complete the exercises that follow it. Directions are provided with each exercise. Correct responses require deliberation and discrimination.

2. Work with students to check their answers. Then discuss the answers with them and have them record the number of correct answers for Part B at the end of the lesson.

Have students study the correct answers to the questions they answered incorrectly. It is important that they understand why a particular answer is correct or incorrect.

Have them reread relevant parts of a passage to clarify an answer. An effective cooperative activity is to have students work in pairs to discuss their answers, explain why they chose the answers they did, and try to resolve differences.

Monitoring Progress

Have students find their total correct answers for the lesson and record their reading time and scores on the graphs on pages 116 and 117. Then have them complete the Comprehension Skills Profile on page 118. For each incorrect response to a question in Part B, students should mark an X in the box above each question type.

The legend on the Reading Rate graph automatically converts reading times to words-per-minute rates. The Comprehension Score graph automatically converts the raw scores to percentages.

These graphs provide a visual record of a student's progress. This record gives the student and you an opportunity to evaluate the student's progress and to determine the types of exercises and skills he or she needs to concentrate on.

Diagnosis and Evaluation

The following are typical reading rates.

Slow Reader—150 Words Per Minute

Average Reader—250 Words Per Minute

Fast Reader—350 Words Per Minute

A student who consistently reads at an average or above-average rate (with satisfactory comprehension) is ready to advance to the next book in the series.

A column of Xs in the Comprehension Skills Profile indicates a specific comprehension weakness. Using the profile, you can assess trends in student performance and suggest remedial work if necessary.

Spending a day at the beach listening to the soothing sounds of ocean waves can be very relaxing. But oceans are not just pleasant places to vacation. Oceans are important to life on Earth. Oceans are part of a delicate ecosystem. An ecosystem is a part of nature in which different things work together as a unified system.

The oceans cover 71 percent of Earth's surface and account for 98 percent of Earth's water. There are five oceans: the Atlantic, the Pacific, the Indian, the Arctic, and the Antarctic. All the oceans are connected, but they are partly divided by continents, such as North America and South America.

Although each ocean is unique, oceans have things in common. All oceans and seas are made up of salt water. Most of the salt in the oceans comes from the erosion of rocks on land. Erosion occurs when rocks wear away and release minerals, such as salt. Water is the cause of most erosion. Rivers transport salt and other minerals to the oceans.

Ninety-nine percent of the salt in the oceans is made up of six substances. The main substance is sodium chloride, which is the type of salt used in salt shakers.

The oceans are vital to life on this planet. They provide us with many resources, including food, energy, and minerals. Fish and shellfish from the oceans are one of our most important food sources. The large deposits of petroleum and natural gas that lie beneath the ocean floors provide energy. Sand and gravel are the primary minerals obtained from the oceans. They are used for making roads and other construction projects.

Plants and animals from the ocean are the source of many types of medicines. For example, a substance in red algae is used to keep blood from clotting. Ocean resources, sometimes called marine resources, have also been helpful in medical research and will continue to help us find new treatments for disease.

Many people are concerned that the ecosystems in oceans can be disrupted when we use marine resources. For example, fishing businesses have to be careful not to catch too many fish so that some species of fish will not become endangered. Removing petroleum from beneath the oceans must be done very carefully to avoid polluting the water. By preserving the ocean ecosystems, we can make sure they will provide resources for future generations.

Reading Time _____

Recalling Facts

1. Oceans make up
   - ❏ a. 25 percent of Earth's surface.
   - ❏ b. 90 percent of Earth's surface.
   - ❏ c. 71 percent of Earth's surface.

2. Oceans are partly divided by
   - ❏ a. continents.
   - ❏ b. the equator.
   - ❏ c. large cities.

3. The main type of salt found in oceans is
   - ❏ a. hydrogen.
   - ❏ b. sodium chloride.
   - ❏ c. magnesium.

4. What are some of the resources found in and below oceans?
   - ❏ a. fish, steel, and ships
   - ❏ b. beef, petroleum, and sand
   - ❏ c. fish, natural gas, and gravel

5. Ninety-eight percent of Earth's water supply is in
   - ❏ a. rivers.
   - ❏ b. the Pacific Ocean.
   - ❏ c. oceans.

Understanding Ideas

6. The article suggests that oceans
   - ❏ a. play a very small role in our lives.
   - ❏ b. contain valuable materials.
   - ❏ c. look bigger than they are.

7. There are probably medicinal plants in the ocean that
   - ❏ a. have not been discovered.
   - ❏ b. have killed many fish.
   - ❏ c. will replace table salt.

8. Why must caution be used when petroleum is moved from ocean floors?
   - ❏ a. There is almost no petroleum left on Earth.
   - ❏ b. Petroleum spills can kill fish and other animals.
   - ❏ c. It is difficult to turn petroleum into gasoline.

9. Why don't oceans contain freshwater?
   - ❏ a. Rivers carry minerals into the ocean.
   - ❏ b. People have removed all the freshwater.
   - ❏ c. Freshwater turns into vapor and rises into the air.

10. You can conclude from the article that if we don't take care of our oceans
   - ❏ a. they will flood the planet.
   - ❏ b. we will damage our ecosystem.
   - ❏ c. they will dry up.

Tide Pools

Tide pools are found along ocean coastlines. They occur where the ocean has worn away rock formations and created small holes. Water accumulates in these holes when the tides move in. Water remains in these holes as the tide recedes, creating pools where many types of sea creatures can live.

Tide pools are difficult to survive in. The water temperature, the amount of water, and the amount of salt in the water are always changing. Tides come in and out twice a day. Waves force water into the tide pools, putting pressure on the creatures that live there. Some of the creatures commonly found in tide pools, such as barnacles, can attach themselves to rocks and are able to survive when the tide pool has little water.

A tide pool can have three parts. The sub-tide zone is always underwater; it is home to seaweed and jellyfish. The mid-tide zone is underwater about half the time and is home to sea anemones, starfish, and clams. The high-tide zone is underwater for only brief periods of time. Crabs and periwinkles live in this zone. A large tide pool that is full of water and has a variety of sea creatures is a fascinating aquarium for the people lucky enough to see it.

1. **Recognizing Words in Context**

   Find the word *accumulates* in the passage. One definition below is closest to the meaning of that word. One definition has the opposite or nearly opposite meaning. The remaining definition has a completely different meaning. Label the definitions C for *closest*, O for *opposite* or *nearly opposite*, and D for *different*.

   _____ a. gathers

   _____ b. invents

   _____ c. disappears

2. **Distinguishing Fact from Opinion**

   Two of the statements below present *facts*, which can be proved correct. The other statement is an *opinion*, which expresses someone's thoughts or beliefs. Label the statements F for *fact* and O for *opinion*.

   _____ a. Tide pools are found along coastlines.

   _____ b. Conditions are often changing in tide pools.

   _____ c. Tide pools are interesting to everyone.

3. Keeping Events in Order

Label each event below as 1, 2, or 3 to show the order in which the events happen.

_____ a. Water fills the holes to form pools.

_____ b. Creatures make their homes in the pools.

_____ c. Holes are created in the rocks by tides.

4. Making Correct Inferences

Two of the statements below are correct *inferences,* or reasonable guesses. They are based on information in the passage. The other statement is an incorrect, or faulty, inference. Label the statements C for *correct* inference and F for *faulty* inference.

_____ a. The amount of salt in the water affects life in a tide pool.

_____ b. The ability to adapt is important for creatures living in tide pools.

_____ c. The tides come in and out at the same time every day.

5. Understanding Main Ideas

One of the statements below expresses the main idea of the passage. One statement is too general, or too broad. The other explains only part of the passage; it is too narrow. Label the statements M for *main idea,* B for *too broad,* and N for *too narrow.*

_____ a. Kelp live in the sub-tide zone.

_____ b. Tide pools are a unique environment for marine life.

_____ c. Oceans are home to a variety of plants and animals.

Correct Answers, Part A _____

Correct Answers, Part B _____

Total Correct Answers _____

16

Computer Games in Education

Technology has dramatically influenced our lives. Education is adapting to meet the changing needs of today's learner. Technology and computer games are now valuable tools in education.

A computer-based learning environment is one in which learners work with information on computers and monitor themselves with little outside supervision. Students determine the problems and work out the answers.

Two types of computer games that work well in classrooms are strategy games and twitch games. In strategy games, the user relies on higher-order thinking skills and problem-solving skills to win. One important higher-order thinking skill is the ability to analyze an unfamiliar situation and make a good decision. The results of the decisions made in a strategy game may not be realized until much later on in the game.

Twitch games provide instant feedback. To win the game, the user must react quickly to situations. Good reflexes and good instincts are the keys to success.

Computer games make students think about problems and solve them in new ways. They must find and remember information. Then they must make it fit into the patterns displayed in the games. Learning how to win a computer game is like learning other skills. It requires a person to find ways to solve problems.

Another skill taught by computer games is how to deal with failure. Getting "lost" in a game world or making wrong decisions that lose the game helps a student to make better decisions in the future. Failure is one of the best ways of learning how to rethink, adapt, and try again. It is one thing for a student to be told that he or she has made a mistake and to be given the right answer. But a much deeper level of learning occurs when the student has to adjust his or her thinking process to figure out why the mistake happened and how to avoid it in the future.

Encouraging students to design new computer games is another way that schools use technology. Students use different kinds of skills to create interesting games that work well. They learn to solve problems, anticipate problems, strategize, and design. Even if the subject of the computer game is not academic, the experience of making the game will help students develop their thinking and problem-solving skills. These skills improve not only the way students learn in school but also the way they learn in the real world.

Reading Time _____

Recalling Facts

1. Dealing with failure is an important skill, because it allows students to
   - ❑ a. adapt and try again.
   - ❑ b. give up.
   - ❑ c. rely on others for the answers.

2. Effective education requires that individual skills be used to
   - ❑ a. solve larger problems.
   - ❑ b. help the student earn money.
   - ❑ c. strengthen research skills.

3. Strategy games rely heavily on
   - ❑ a. the speed of the computer.
   - ❑ b. advanced problem-solving skills.
   - ❑ c. hand-eye coordination.

4. A person who does well at twitch games is most likely to have
   - ❑ a. good reflexes.
   - ❑ b. extremely high intelligence.
   - ❑ c. problems with logic.

5. The results of a decision made in a strategy game
   - ❑ a. have no effect on the game.
   - ❑ b. are immediately apparent.
   - ❑ c. may not be realized until later in the game.

Understanding Ideas

6. When students work in a computer-based learning environment, they
   - ❑ a. work together as a full class to solve problems.
   - ❑ b. work with information while supervising themselves.
   - ❑ c. design games while working one-on-one with the teacher.

7. You could assume that designing a good computer game
   - ❑ a. takes a lot of patience and determination.
   - ❑ b. is an easy assignment that anyone can do.
   - ❑ c. does not have much educational value.

8. Which of the following statements is not true?
   - ❑ a. Computer games teach problem-solving techniques.
   - ❑ b. Computer games strengthen thinking skills.
   - ❑ c. Computer games have no educational benefit.

9. Skills learned from computer games
   - ❑ a. are not beneficial to students.
   - ❑ b. help students in both academic and life settings.
   - ❑ c. do not teach students about the real world.

10. It is safe to assume that
    - ❑ a. computer games do not provide the user with helpful skills.
    - ❑ b. computers will be even more helpful in education in the future.
    - ❑ c. computer technology has not improved education.

How to Be a Game Programmer

The most important characteristic for a computer game programmer is a love of games. You must also love breaking a game down into its smallest parts and seeing how the parts fit into a whole. You must have creative problem-solving skills.

A computer game passes through many hands before it makes it to the store shelf. But the most critical job is that of the programmer. If you want to be a game programmer, you need to learn a computer language. The most popular languages are C and C++, but any computer language will work as long as you know it well. You will also need a compiler. A compiler is a computer program that changes a computer language used by humans into a language that a computer can execute, or perform.

The best way to begin a career as a computer game programmer is to write a game. Write one as soon as possible. It doesn't have to be a good game. It doesn't have to be a complex game. It just needs to work. You can use this first game as a stepping-stone for your next game. Your first computer game is part of your learning curve.

Continue to play games. Learn computer languages. Imagine complex story lines. And most importantly, have fun!

1. **Recognizing Words in Context**

   Find the word *critical* in the passage. One definition below is closest to the meaning of that word. One definition has the opposite or nearly opposite meaning. The remaining definition has a completely different meaning. Label the definitions C for *closest,* O for *opposite or nearly opposite,* and D for *different.*

   _____ a. unimportant

   _____ b. essential

   _____ c. new

2. **Distinguishing Fact from Opinion**

   Two of the statements below present *facts,* which can be proved correct. The other statement is an *opinion,* which expresses someone's thoughts or beliefs. Label the statements F for *fact* and O for *opinion.*

   _____ a. A game programmer must have problem-solving skills.

   _____ b. A game programmer must know a computer language.

   _____ c. If you love computer games, you'll be a great programmer.

3. Keeping Events in Order

Label the statements below 1, 2, and 3 to show the order in which the events would happen.

_____ a. You learn a computer language.

_____ b. You gain problem-solving skills over a period of years.

_____ c. You design your first computer game.

4. Making Correct Inferences

Two of the statements below are correct *inferences,* or reasonable guesses. They are based on information in the passage. The other statement is an incorrect, or faulty, inference. Label the statements C for *correct* inference and F for *faulty* inference.

_____ a. If you enjoy playing games, you might enjoy a career as a game programmer.

_____ b. To create games, it is important to be proficient in a computer language.

_____ c. Learning to become a game programmer is fairly easy and requires a week of training.

5. Understanding Main Ideas

One of the statements below expresses the main idea of the passage. One statement is too general, or too broad. The other explains only part of the passage; it is too narrow. Label the statements M for *main idea,* B for *too broad,* and N for *too narrow.*

_____ a. A career as a computer-game programmer utilizes many skills.

_____ b. A game programmer should have a compiler.

_____ c. The computer industry provides many career opportunities.

Correct Answers, Part A _____

Correct Answers, Part B _____

Total Correct Answers _____

The Rock Cycle

People use rocks in many ways. Some people decorate their gardens with them. Others keep them as pets. Construction companies use rocks to build things. But where do rocks come from? Rocks are actually produced as part of a process called the rock cycle. The process of creating rocks depends on such things as temperature, pressure, and time.

There are three types of rock: igneous, sedimentary, and metamorphic. Igneous rocks form when molten material such as lava cools and solidifies, or changes into a solid. This process is called crystallization. Most of Earth is made up of igneous rock.

There are two main types of igneous rock: intrusive and extrusive. Intrusive igneous rocks solidify beneath Earth's surface. They often contain a variety of minerals and have a rough texture. Granite is a good example of this type of rock. Extrusive rocks solidify on Earth's surface. Molten material inside Earth is called magma. When magma comes to the surface, it flows out as lava. Lava solidifies quickly because Earth's surface is much cooler than Earth's core. Basalt is an example of extrusive igneous rock.

Sedimentary rocks form when sediments—tiny particles of matter such as sand, gravel, and shells—are carried off by wind or water. For example, as a river flows over rocks, it wears away particles of the rocks. These particles are carried away as sediment and are deposited in places where the river flows more slowly. Sediment deposits form layers called strata. As water circulates around the layers, the sediment is cemented together to form rocks. Sedimentary rocks are the softest and least brittle of all the rock types.

Metamorphic rocks form when igneous or sedimentary rocks are changed by heat or pressure. Heat or pressure causes rock to recrystallize and form different mineral substances with different textures.

All of these ways in which rock forms are part of the rock cycle. It is also possible for rocks to change from one type to another. For example, igneous rock can change to sedimentary rock or metamorphic rock, and sedimentary rock can change to metamorphic rock or igneous rock. Rocks are constantly changing as part of this cycle. You might enjoy learning more about rocks by using books to help you identify interesting rocks that you find. With experience, you can become a first-class "rock hound," and you may even find something valuable!

Reading Time _____

Recalling Facts

1. Most of Earth is made up of
   - ❏ a. sedimentary rock.
   - ❏ b. igneous rock.
   - ❏ c. metamorphic rock.

2. Extrusive igneous rock is formed from
   - ❏ a. molten lava.
   - ❏ b. mineral deposits.
   - ❏ c. fossils.

3. The series of changes that rocks go through is called
   - ❏ a. erosion.
   - ❏ b. evolution.
   - ❏ c. the rock cycle.

4. Sediments are most commonly carried
   - ❏ a. by insects or animals.
   - ❏ b. in trucks or trains.
   - ❏ c. by water or wind.

5. Layers of sediment are called
   - ❏ a. strata.
   - ❏ b. lava.
   - ❏ c. basalt.

Understanding Ideas

6. Compared with sedimentary rocks, igneous rocks would most likely be
   - ❏ a. smoother
   - ❏ b. rougher.
   - ❏ c. smaller.

7. You could assume that most of the rock types around a volcano are
   - ❏ a. igneous.
   - ❏ b. sedimentary.
   - ❏ c. metamorphic.

8. A good place to find sedimentary rocks would probably be
   - ❏ a. in a lake.
   - ❏ b. in a forest.
   - ❏ c. on a mountain.

9. Extrusive rocks solidify quickly because of the
   - ❏ a. speed at which they exit Earth's core.
   - ❏ b. combination of mineral deposits in the soil.
   - ❏ c. large difference in temperature between Earth's core and its surface.

10. The article suggests that the rock cycle
    - ❏ a. has a beginning and an ending.
    - ❏ b. is always in motion.
    - ❏ c. occurs only in water.

Caitlin and her mother arrived at Bryce Canyon National Park in Utah.

"It's incredible, isn't it?" said Caitlin's mother.

"How was it made?" Caitlin asked.

"Millions of years of erosion created these rock formations," her mother explained. "A huge lake formed here more than 100 million years ago and began wearing away the rock." She thumbed through her travel brochure. "It says here that the sediments carried and deposited by water became thousands of feet thick. The different minerals from the sediments created the variety of colors you see."

Caitlin saw the smoky gray rocks at the base of the canyon. She pointed to ridges and spires that seemed to be coming out of the rocks. "What are those?"

"Those are called hoodoos. They are also formed from erosion. The ridges of the rocks slowly eroded away to become these fantastic shapes that we see today."

"What else does it say?"

"It says Bryce Canyon isn't actually a canyon. It's a group of amphitheaters that have been carved by erosion. Amphitheaters are level areas that are surrounded by steep slopes."

Some of the rock formations looked deep red or purple and blue in the setting sun. Her mother pointed to the Pink Cliffs. "The color in those rocks came from iron particles in the rocks that oxidized over time."

Caitlin was in awe of the spectacular display of color. "When we get home, I'd like to read to find out the differences between Bryce Canyon and the Grand Canyon," she said.

1. Recognizing Words in Context

Find the word *erosion* in the passage. One definition below is closest to the meaning of that word. One definition has the opposite or nearly opposite meaning. The remaining definition has a completely different meaning. Label the definitions C for *closest,* O for *opposite or nearly opposite,* and D for *different.*

_____ a. wearing away

_____ b. adding to

_____ c. driving straight

2. Distinguishing Fact from Opinion

Two of the statements below present *facts,* which can be proved correct. The other statement is an *opinion,* which expresses someone's thoughts or beliefs. Label the statements F for *fact* and O for *opinion.*

_____ a. Erosion caused many of the rock formations found in Bryce Canyon.

_____ b. The Pink Cliffs get their color from iron deposits.

_____ c. Bryce Canyon is one of the most beautiful places on Earth.

3. Keeping Events in Order

Label the statements below 1, 2, and 3 to show the order in which the events happened.

_____ a. Layers of sediment formed into rocks.

_____ b. Water began to deposit the sediments that formed Bryce Canyon.

_____ c. The ridges of the rocks eroded to form hoodoos.

4. Making Correct Inferences

Two of the statements below are correct *inferences,* or reasonable guesses. They are based on information in the passage. The other statement is an incorrect, or faulty, inference. Label the statements C for *correct* inference and F for *faulty* inference.

_____ a. After another 100 million years, Bryce Canyon will look different than it does today.

_____ b. Sediments deposited from water always form the same color patterns.

_____ c. Erosion created many of the landforms we see today.

5. Understanding Main Ideas

One of the statements below expresses the main idea of the passage. One statement is too general, or too broad. The other explains only part of the passage; it is too narrow. Label the statements M for *main idea,* B for *too broad,* and N for *too narrow.*

_____ a. Bryce Canyon consists of beautiful and unusual rock formations.

_____ b. Hoodoos are the ridges that appear to be coming out of the rocks.

_____ c. Erosion is part of our planet's history.

Correct Answers, Part A _____

Correct Answers, Part B _____

Total Correct Answers _____

What Is Hail?

Hail is frozen rain that falls to the ground during a thunderstorm. The first requirement of a good hailstorm is cumulonimbus clouds. Cumulonimbus clouds are very high, dark, thick clouds. They usually bring thunderstorms.

A hailstone is an ice pellet that is shaped like a sphere. As rain begins to fall to Earth from within cumulonimbus clouds, the raindrops are caught in a strong upward wind current called an updraft. As they are thrown back up into the cold air at the top of the cloud, they freeze and start to fall to Earth again. Sometimes the frozen raindrops get caught in the updraft again and are tossed back to the top of the clouds, where additional layers of ice cover them. The stronger the updraft, the larger the hailstone will be. Eventually, the weight of the hailstone becomes heavy enough to allow it to fall through the updraft. Hailstones range in size from 1 to 14 centimeters (⅜ inch to 5½ inches) in diameter, and they can weigh as much as 730 grams (1⅗ pounds). Smaller pellets of hail are known as sleet. When the hailstones fall to Earth, they can reach speeds of 100 kph (60 mph) for a 4-centimeter (1½ inch) stone.

The column of air through which hailstones fall to the ground is called the hail shaft. The ground area that is swept by the hailstorm is called the hail streak. Hail streaks can range from 30 meters to 3.2 kilometers (100 feet to 2 miles) wide, and they average 8 kilometers (5 miles) in length. Generally hailstorms occur in the mid- or late afternoon and last for about 15 minutes. The majority of hailstorms in the United States occur in an area of the Great Plains known as Hail Alley. Many of these storms occur in May or June. Cheyenne, Wyoming, is considered the hailstorm capital of the world. It has an average of 10 storms each year. Florida has the fewest hailstorms in the United States.

Hailstorms occur in the summer or winter months. People often wonder how rain can be frozen during the middle of summer. This is because the air that is high up in a cumulonimbus cloud is much cooler than the air on the ground. When a rapidly moving cold front moves into an area, the weather can change dramatically. As a result, warm summer weather can turn into a hailstorm in a matter of minutes.

Reading Time _____

Recalling Facts

1. A hailstone is a sphere-shaped pellet of
   - ❏ a. melted snow.
   - ❏ b. frozen rain.
   - ❏ c. icy vapor.

2. The column of air through which hailstones fall to Earth is called the
   - ❏ a. hailstorm.
   - ❏ b. hail streak.
   - ❏ c. hail shaft.

3. The ground area that is swept by a hailstorm is called the
   - ❏ a. hail alley.
   - ❏ b. hail stone.
   - ❏ c. hail streak.

4. Hailstorms generally last for about
   - ❏ a. 30 minutes.
   - ❏ b. 15 minutes.
   - ❏ c. 60 minutes.

5. The hailstorm capital of the world is
   - ❏ a. Cheyenne, Wyoming.
   - ❏ b. Charleston, South Carolina.
   - ❏ c. Lincoln, Nebraska.

Understanding Ideas

6. If you see cumulonimbus clouds in the sky, it is likely that
   - ❏ a. you will see a rainbow.
   - ❏ b. the day will be clear.
   - ❏ c. a storm is approaching.

7. If a hailstone falls to the ground, you can assume that the weight of the stone was large enough that the force of gravity was _____ the force of the updraft.
   - ❏ a. equal to
   - ❏ b. less than
   - ❏ c. greater than

8. Which of the following statements is not true?
   - ❏ a. Hailstorms can always be predicted.
   - ❏ b. Hailstones vary in size.
   - ❏ c. Hailstones can be damaging.

9. If you notice ice bouncing on the street in a Plains state in August, you are probably witnessing a
   - ❏ a. blizzard.
   - ❏ b. hailstorm.
   - ❏ c. hurricane.

10. You can conclude from the article that weather conditions in the United States
    - ❏ a. vary.
    - ❏ b. are the same in the East and the West.
    - ❏ c. are the same all over the West, but not the East.

The Sky Is Falling!

It was September 3, 1970, in the small town of Coffeyville, Kansas. As the day progressed, cumulus clouds began gathering in the sky. A storm had been forecast. Soon the darker cumulonimbus clouds appeared. The townspeople watched the approaching thunderstorm. The winds blew stronger, and the storm began. But this wasn't just a thunderstorm. It was a hailstorm!

The ice pellets bounced when they hit the pavement. The hail clattered over the roofs of cars and buildings. People moved indoors to wait out the storm. Some hailstones were so large it was frightening. One hailstone measured 43 centimeters (17½ inches) in circumference and 14 centimeters (5½ inches) in diameter. It weighed 730 grams (1⅗ pounds)! This was the largest hailstone ever recorded in the United States.

It would have taken an extremely strong updraft to toss the hailstone repeatedly up into the top of a cloud and form a hailstone the size of a football. When people in Coffeyville cut the hailstone in half, they could see many separate layers of ice.

Fortunately this hailstone did not injure anyone. Hailstones have killed only two people in the United States. However, hailstones can cause damage to people, livestock, and property. If you find yourself caught in a hailstorm, find shelter as quickly as possible. Watch the storm from the safety of your home!

1. **Recognizing Words in Context**

Find the word *clattered* in the passage. One definition below is closest to the meaning of that word. One definition has the opposite or nearly opposite meaning. The remaining definition has a completely different meaning. Label the definitions C for *closest*, O for *opposite or nearly opposite*, and D for *different*.

_____ a. rattled

_____ b. removed

_____ c. softly touched

2. **Distinguishing Fact from Opinion**

Two of the statements below present *facts*, which can be proved correct. The other statement is an *opinion*, which expresses someone's thoughts or beliefs. Label the statements F for *fact* and O for *opinion*.

_____ a. No one will ever be killed from a hailstone again.

_____ b. The largest hailstone in the United States fell in Coffeyville, Kansas.

_____ c. Hailstorms can cause property damage.

3. Keeping Events in Order

Label the statements below 1, 2, and 3 to show the order in which the events happened.

_____ a. Cumulus clouds began gathering.

_____ b. Large hailstones fell from the sky.

_____ c. Cumulonimbus clouds appeared.

4. Making Correct Inferences

Two of the statements below are correct *inferences*, or reasonable guesses. They are based on information in the passage. The other statement is an incorrect, or faulty, inference. Label the statements C for *correct* inference and F for *faulty* inference.

_____ a. The larger a hailstone is, the more times it was tossed into the clouds by an updraft.

_____ b. The hailstone measured at Coffeyville, Kansas, is as large as one can get.

_____ c. You can get hurt if you are outside during a hailstorm.

5. Understanding Main Ideas

One of the statements below expresses the main idea of the passage. One statement is too general, or too broad. The other explains only part of the passage; it is too narrow. Label the statements M for *main idea*, B for *too broad*, and N for *too narrow*.

_____ a. The hailstone that fell in Coffeyville weighed 1.67 pounds.

_____ b. Hailstones can be very large.

_____ c. The largest hailstone recorded in the United States fell in Kansas.

Correct Answers, Part A _____

Correct Answers, Part B _____

Total Correct Answers _____

Every creature in nature, from the smallest single-cell organism to a human being, plays a role in how ecosystems work. If one species becomes extinct, species throughout the world may be affected.

Every living thing is food for another living thing. A food chain shows the order in which living things are eaten by other living things in an ecological community. Each member of the food chain passes on energy and nutrients to the next member. For example, an earthworm may be food for a robin, and a robin may be food for a cat.

Within each food chain, there are predators and prey. Predators survive by eating other living things. A cat is a predator. It feeds on smaller animals such as birds and mice. These animals are the cat's prey.

Each species occupies a certain position in a food chain, but a species may be in different positions in different food chains. For example, a fish might be at the top of one food chain that shows smaller insects being eaten by larger insects, and larger insects being eaten by the fish. But the fish might be at the bottom of another food chain in which seals eat fish, and polar bears eat seals.

Food chains are made up of producers, consumers, and decomposers. Producers are capable of making their own food. They are often at the bottom of a food chain. Green plants are our most important producers. They use a combination of sunlight, minerals, and gases to produce food within themselves.

Consumers are creatures that can't produce food within themselves. They have to eat other livings things or food made by other things. There are three types of consumers: herbivores, carnivores, and omnivores. Herbivores eat plants. Carnivores eat meat. Omnivores eat both plants and meat. Humans are an example of omnivores, although some humans choose not to eat meat.

Decomposers break down organic compounds in dead animals. They release raw materials, such as carbon dioxide, back into the environment. Fungi and bacteria are important decomposers.

Food chains are part of larger groupings called food webs. Some animals eat many kinds of plants and animals, and these animals may be eaten by several kinds of larger animals. They are parts of many different chains. These chains can be connected by a food web, which gives a more complex and accurate picture of the feeding relationships in nature.

Reading Time _____

Recalling Facts

1. What shows the feeding relationships between living things?
   - ❏ a. predators
   - ❏ b. food chains
   - ❏ c. plant species

2. Consumers are not able to
   - ❏ a. produce food within themselves.
   - ❏ b. get enough to eat.
   - ❏ c. survive in the winter.

3. The most important producers in our ecosystem are
   - ❏ a. fish.
   - ❏ b. lions.
   - ❏ c. green plants.

4. Decomposers include
   - ❏ a. bacteria.
   - ❏ b. seeds.
   - ❏ c. insects.

5. Creatures that eat only plants are called
   - ❏ a. carnivores.
   - ❏ b. herbivores.
   - ❏ c. omnivores.

Understanding Ideas

6. Which of these statements represents an accurate conclusion?
   - ❏ a. All plants and animals can live in the same region.
   - ❏ b. An earthquake has no effect on the environment.
   - ❏ c. Living things are food for other living things.

7. Because a zebra passes on energy and nutrients to a lion, you can assume that they are
   - ❏ a. members of the same food chain.
   - ❏ b. omnivores.
   - ❏ c. of the same species.

8. Green plants are often the first level of a food chain because they
   - ❏ a. require less food to survive.
   - ❏ b. are able to support the rest of the chain.
   - ❏ c. are able to live longer.

9. You could conclude that if several members of a food chain vanished,
   - ❏ a. nothing would change.
   - ❏ b. other members of the food chain would be affected.
   - ❏ c. there would be more herbivores.

10. The main lesson you can learn from the article about food chains is that
    - ❏ a. consumers are more important than decomposers.
    - ❏ b. producers are more important than consumers.
    - ❏ c. all groups are equally important.

Fungus Farmers

Ants are known for the complex social structures of their colonies. But one type of ant has an especially advanced way of living. The leaf-cutter ant of South America actually grows its own food. Most ant species gather food to bring back to the colony. The leaf-cutter ant, however, devotes much of its time to growing fungus.

Scientists are not clear how this trait developed. One theory is that the ants were simply poor housekeepers. Fungus might have grown on seeds and plant materials that the ants had stored away. Over time, the ants might have begun to depend on the fungus for food.

These fungus-growing ants devote lots of time and energy to gathering the plants they use to grow their fungus gardens. A leaf-cutter ant chews off a section of a leaf and brings the section back to its colony. There, other ants chew the leaf sections into tiny pieces and pile them in a moist mass. Over time, fungus grows on the mass of leaf pieces. The ants allow only one type of fungus to grow in their colonies; they remove other types. Some types of fungi that grow in the ant colonies are not found anywhere else in the world! The leaf-cutter ant's method of obtaining food is one of the most unusual in the insect world.

1. **Recognizing Words in Context**

   Find the word *complex* in the passage. One definition below is closest to the meaning of that word. One definition has the opposite or nearly opposite meaning. The remaining definition has a completely different meaning. Label the definitions C for *closest*, O for *opposite or nearly opposite,* and D for *different*.

   _____ a. complicated

   _____ b. electronic

   _____ c. simple

2. **Distinguishing Fact from Opinion**

   Two of the statements below present *facts,* which can be proved correct. The other statement is an *opinion,* which expresses someone's thoughts or beliefs. Label the statements F for *fact* and O for *opinion*.

   _____ a. Some types of fungi are found only in ant colonies.

   _____ b. Leaf-cutter ants are the most amazing ants.

   _____ c. Leaf-cutter ants need fungus to survive.

3. Keeping Events in Order

Label the statements below 1, 2, and 3 to show the order in which the events happen.

_____ a. Fungus grows from chewed leaves.

_____ b. Ants chew leaf sections into tiny pieces.

_____ c. Ants leave the colony to gather leaf material.

4. Making Correct Inferences

Two of the statements below are correct *inferences*, or reasonable guesses. They are based on information in the passage. The other statement is an incorrect, or faulty, inference. Label the statements C for *correct* inference and F for *faulty* inference.

_____ a. Growing fungus is one of the most important activities of leaf-cutter ants.

_____ b. If fungus did not grow, leaf-cutter ants would find another way to survive.

_____ c. Without leaves, leaf-cutter ants would not be able to grow enough food.

5. Understanding Main Ideas

One of the statements below expresses the main idea of the passage. One statement is too general, or too broad. The other explains only part of the passage; it is too narrow. Label the statements M for *main idea,* B for *too broad,* and N for *too narrow.*

_____ a. Ants are one of the most advanced forms of insect life.

_____ b. Leaf-cutter ants eat just one type of fungus.

_____ c. Leaf-cutter ants have an interesting way of getting food.

Correct Answers, Part A _____

Correct Answers, Part B _____

Total Correct Answers _____

The Work of an Archaeologist

An archaeologist is someone who studies past cultures. A culture consists of the ideas, customs, skills, beliefs, and arts of a specific people during a specific time period. We can learn about our own culture by studying the cultures of the past. One goal of archaeologists is to learn how different groups fulfilled some of the same basic needs we have today: food, shelter, and clothing. Archaeologists can do this by studying artifacts, which are objects made by the people of a particular culture.

The three main duties of an archaeologist are to observe, to discover, and to record. Archaeologists often work for museums or universities. They study both prehistoric and historic sites. A prehistoric site is a place that existed before humans kept written records. A historic site is a site that was occupied after humans began keeping written records. A site can be a single building or a small area. It can also be a whole village.

Two key parts of an archaeologist's job are research and education. Research begins with a curiosity about something in the past. For instance, suppose you were an archaeologist and you wondered about the type of pottery used in the Roman city of Pompeii before Mount Vesuvius erupted in A.D. 79. First, you would pose a question about the pottery. Then you would set out to find information. You might help excavate a site. Or you might study artifacts that are in a museum, such as the one in Naples, Italy.

You would use the findings from your research to form conclusions and answer your question. You would report your findings and conclusions to the scientific community. This is the education part of an archaeologist's job.

If you want to become an archaeologist, you should have an interest in history and science. In school, you should study anthropology and biology. An interest in zoology and geology would be helpful too. You'll need to know how to identify prehistoric artifacts, bones, and types of rocks. All of this specific information will lead up to an understanding of a culture and its people.

An archaeologist's discoveries can greatly change the way people view history. For example, in the mid-1900s, Louis and Mary Leakey found fossils in eastern Africa that showed that the human species had developed much earlier than people had thought. Important archaeological discoveries can help us better understand our history—and also ourselves.

Reading Time _____

33

Recalling Facts

1. An archaeologist studies
   - ❏ a. language.
   - ❏ b. cultures.
   - ❏ c. weather patterns.

2. An object made by the people of a past culture is called an
   - ❏ a. excavation.
   - ❏ b. abyss.
   - ❏ c. artifact.

3. A site that existed before humans kept written records is called a
   - ❏ a. prehistoric site.
   - ❏ b. historic site.
   - ❏ c. current site.

4. The skills, beliefs, arts, and customs of a specific people in a specific time is a
   - ❏ a. memory.
   - ❏ b. culture.
   - ❏ c. family.

5. The three main parts of an archaeologist's job are to
   - ❏ a. invent, to write, and to travel.
   - ❏ b. create, to explore, and to share.
   - ❏ c. observe, to discover, and to record.

Understanding Ideas

6. Archaeologists study artifacts mainly to
   - ❏ a. put together a museum exhibit.
   - ❏ b. learn more about a culture.
   - ❏ c. understand climate changes.

7. After an archaeologist completes a research study, it is likely that
   - ❏ a. the study will be of little interest to other archaeologists.
   - ❏ b. archaeologists will think of new questions to ask.
   - ❏ c. the archaeologist will lose interest in the topic.

8. Which of the following statements is not true?
   - ❏ a. Archaeologists study past cultures.
   - ❏ b. Archaeologists may work for a museum.
   - ❏ c. All archaeologists work on excavating historic sites.

9. You can conclude from the article that an archaeologist
   - ❏ a. needs many different kinds of skills.
   - ❏ b. must live near a university.
   - ❏ c. always finds work in a museum.

10. Which of these characteristics would be least useful to an archaeologist?
    - ❏ a. a need for quick results
    - ❏ b. an eye for detail
    - ❏ c. curiosity about the past

The Process of an Archaeological Dig

The most valuable way that archaeologists can answer important questions concerning past cultures is by finding new evidence. They can do this by uncovering artifacts during a process known as a dig. A successful dig requires careful planning and detailed work.

When a team of archaeologists believes there may be reason to dig at a certain location, they first plot the site. This means they map out its exact location. Then they obtain a license to excavate from the proper government agency. When they have the license, they survey the site and make a grid of it. They remove the sod and topsoil with shovels and begin the dig. Digging takes a great deal of physical effort. The diggers must be careful not to damage anything found on the site. Much of the work is done with dental picks, paintbrushes, and tiny shovels called trowels.

Everything dug up is analyzed and recorded. Larger artifacts are left where they were found until the whole area is uncovered. Photographs are taken during every step of the digging process. Correctly following this process ensures that the findings are accurate and that the site is cared for and preserved for others. After archaeologists complete the dig, they study their findings and draw conclusions. They publish these conclusions in scientific journals or other publications.

1. **Recognizing Words in Context**

Find the word *excavate* in the passage. One definition below is closest to the meaning of that word. One definition has the opposite or nearly opposite meaning. The remaining definition has a completely different meaning. Label the definitions C for *closest,* O for *opposite or nearly opposite,* and D for *different.*

_____ a. paint

_____ b. dig up

_____ c. bury

2. **Distinguishing Fact from Opinion**

Two of the statements below present *facts,* which can be proved correct. The other statement is an *opinion,* which expresses someone's thoughts or beliefs. Label the statements F for *fact* and O for *opinion.*

_____ a. Finding buried treasures is the best part of an archaeological dig.

_____ b. An archaeological dig is a precise process.

_____ c. Artifacts found in archaeological digs are preserved for future research.

3. Keeping Events in Order

Label the statements below 1, 2, and 3 to show the order in which the events happen.

_____ a. Archaeologists think of a question to research.

_____ b. Archaeologists obtain a license from an agency.

_____ c. Archaeologists decide where to dig.

4. Making Correct Inferences

Two of the statements below are correct *inferences,* or reasonable guesses. They are based on information in the passage. The other statement is an incorrect, or faulty, inference. Label the statements C for *correct* inference and F for *faulty* inference.

_____ a. Archaeologists' work is often slow and difficult.

_____ b. Archaeologists are always very athletic.

_____ c. Archaeologists pay close attention to details.

5. Understanding Main Ideas

One of the statements below expresses the main idea of the passage. One statement is too general, or too broad. The other explains only part of the passage; it is too narrow. Label the statements M for *main idea,* B for *too broad,* and N for *too narrow.*

_____ a. Archaeologists dig with trowels.

_____ b. Archaeologists possess a variety of skills.

_____ c. An archaeological dig is a precise process.

Correct Answers, Part A _____

Correct Answers, Part B _____

Total Correct Answers _____

Hans Christian Oersted, a Danish scientist, accidentally discovered the connection between electricity and magnetism in 1820. One day he was setting up an experiment alongside a compass that was lying on a table. Oersted found that when he sent electricity through a wire, it made his compass needle move away from the north position. A compass needle normally points north, because Earth's magnetic pole is near the North Pole. His compass did not point north as it should have, so he knew that something strange had occurred. Oersted concluded that running electric current through a wire makes the wire magnetic.

The type of magnet that Oersted discovered is called an electromagnet. It is similar to a permanent magnet, the kind that you may have on your refrigerator. The only difference is that a permanent magnet always has a charge. An electromagnet's charge is temporary. An area with magnetic force, called a magnetic field, exists only when electricity is present. This means that the magnet can be turned on and off.

An electromagnet must have a source of electricity. One such source is a battery. A battery produces negative particles called electrons, which are what create electric current. The electrons gather at the negative end of the battery. If the electrons move, they flow from the negative end to the positive end through a wire. A wire attached between the positive and the negative end of a battery makes a path that allows the electrons to flow. The electrons move quickly along this path. As they travel, the electrons create a small magnetic field.

In this simple type of an electromagnet, the battery wears out very fast. However, if the wire in an electromagnet is coiled, a stronger magnetic field is created. If the wire is coiled around an iron object, such as a nail, the magnetic field is even stronger.

One common example of how an electromagnet works is found in some car horns. These horns have two main parts. One is a thin metal disk called a diaphragm, and the other is an electromagnet. When someone pushes the steering wheel to honk the horn, an electric current flowing to the electro-magnet causes the diaphragm to vibrate, which creates the sound of the horn. The sound varies depending on the type of metal in the diaphragm. Other common examples of electromagnets can be found in doorbells, stereo speakers, television sets, and car engines.

Reading Time _____

Recalling Facts

1. Oersted discovered the connection between electricity and magnetism in
   - ❏ a. 1850.
   - ❏ b. 1820.
   - ❏ c. 1920.

2. A battery is an example of a
   - ❏ a. power source.
   - ❏ b. magnet.
   - ❏ c. computer.

3. Electric current running through a wire creates
   - ❏ a. a chemical reaction.
   - ❏ b. static electricity.
   - ❏ c. a magnetic field.

4. A battery produces
   - ❏ a. electrons.
   - ❏ b. neutrons.
   - ❏ c. protons.

5. Which of the following devices uses an electromagnet?
   - ❏ a. a gas grill
   - ❏ b. a speaker
   - ❏ c. a flashlight

Understanding Ideas

6. For electrons to flow from the negative end to the positive end of a battery, there must be a
   - ❏ a. switch.
   - ❏ b. job.
   - ❏ c. path.

7. An electromagnet works only when
   - ❏ a. the electric current is stopped.
   - ❏ b. the electric current is flowing.
   - ❏ c. it is attached to a motor.

8. An electromagnet's magnetic field can be made stronger by
   - ❏ a. uncoiling the wire.
   - ❏ b. coiling wire around a nail.
   - ❏ c. placing the battery in the sun.

9. If a compass needle is pointing away from magnetic north, you can assume you are
   - ❏ a. near an electromagnet field.
   - ❏ b. near water.
   - ❏ c. walking in the wrong direction.

10. One advantage of using electromagnets is that
    - ❏ a. their charge is permanent.
    - ❏ b. they are made of wood.
    - ❏ c. we can turn them on and off when we want to.

Electricity's Journey

Electricity is the flow of energy from one place to another. Its path to your house is long and complex. Electricity isn't made within the walls of a house. It is generated at a large power plant. At most power plants, a fuel source, such as coal or oil, is burned to produce steam. The steam passes through a machine called a turbine. The turbine produces electricity in a device called a generator. Once electricity is produced, it is transmitted to local utilities through high-voltage power lines. The local utility then delivers the electricity to homes and businesses. This delivery is called distribution.

Inside the walls of a house are mazes of wires. These wires make up circuits. Most wires are made of copper. Copper is a good conductor of electricity. Each circuit begins and ends at a circuit box. All electricity enters and leaves the home through the circuit box. Switches on the walls allow the electrical flow to be controlled. The switch opens and closes a gap in the circuit. Electricity cannot flow through the gap. Circuit breakers keep too much electricity from flowing through a circuit. When there is too much electricity, the circuit breaker flips to the "off" position. This makes a gap in the circuit. Circuit breakers are very important, because too much electricity flowing through a wire can melt the wire and cause a fire.

1. Recognizing Words in Context

Find the word *transmitted* in the passage. One definition below is closest to the meaning of that word. One definition has the opposite or nearly opposite meaning. The remaining definition has a completely different meaning. Label the definitions C for *closest*, O for *opposite or nearly opposite,* and D for *different.*

_____ a. brought in

_____ b. sent out

_____ c. discussed

2. Distinguishing Fact from Opinion

Two of the statements below present *facts,* which can be proved correct. The other statement is an *opinion,* which expresses someone's thoughts or beliefs. Label the statements F for *fact* and O for *opinion.*

_____ a. Electricity is necessary for a comfortable life.

_____ b. Electricity can be generated from a fuel source.

_____ c. Electricity flows through wires.

3. **Keeping Events in Order**

Label the statements below 1, 2, and 3 to show the order in which the events happen.

_____ a. The circuit breaker flips to "off" position.

_____ b. Electricity flows to the wires in a house.

_____ c. Electricity is generated at a power plant.

4. **Making Correct Inferences**

Two of the statements below are correct *inferences*, or reasonable guesses. They are based on information in the passage. The other statement is an incorrect, or faulty, inference. Label the statements C for *correct* inference and F for *faulty* inference.

_____ a. All electricity comes from power plants that burn fuel.

_____ b. Generating electricity is very important to people.

_____ c. Copper wiring is often used during the construction of a house.

5. **Understanding Main Ideas**

One of the statements below expresses the main idea of the passage. One statement is too general, or too broad. The other explains only part of the passage; it is too narrow. Label the statements M for *main idea*, B for *too broad*, and N for *too narrow*.

_____ a. Electricity is energy flow.

_____ b. Electricity goes through many steps before it is used in a home.

_____ c. Circuit breakers can prevent fires.

Correct Answers, Part A _____

Correct Answers, Part B _____

Total Correct Answers _____

Water Properties

Earth is the only planet known to have water. Water covers about 70 percent of Earth's surface. It also makes up about 75 percent of a human being's body weight. There are two kinds of water: freshwater and salt water. Ninety-seven percent of all the water on Earth is in the oceans as salt water. Although humans cannot drink salt water, it provides the perfect environment for many kinds of fish and plant life. All living things need water. It is vital in biological systems, such as the digestive system and the circulatory system.

Water is the most common compound on Earth. The water molecule is made up of two atoms of hydrogen and one atom of oxygen (H_2O). Water has several unique properties. It occurs commonly in all three states of matter: solid, liquid, and gas. It freezes at 0 degrees Celsius (32 degrees Fahrenheit) and boils at 100 degrees Celsius (212 degrees Fahrenheit). Unlike any other substance on Earth, water actually expands when it freezes. The reason ice floats in a glass of water or other liquid is that the expansion of the water molecules makes the ice less dense than the liquid in which it is floating.

One of the interesting properties of water is its buoyancy. Buoyancy is the tendency of an object to float. More than 2,000 years ago, a Greek mathematician named Archimedes discovered that an object weighs less in water than in air. You may have noticed this if you have ever been in a swimming pool with a friend. In the water, you can lift someone that you are unable to lift on land. This happens because when an object is placed in water, the water around the object pushes upward. It pushes upward with a force that is equal to the weight of the water that was displaced, or moved out of the way, when the object entered the water. Objects that are less dense than water will float.

Water pressure increases with the depth of the water. You can see this easily for yourself. If you fill a plastic bottle with water and cut two equally sized holes in it at different levels, the water will flow more forcefully from the lower hole.

Understanding the properties of water is important because water is critical to life on Earth. The more we know about water, the more wisely we can use it.

Reading Time _____

Recalling Facts

1. When water freezes, it
   - ❏ a. contracts.
   - ❏ b. expands.
   - ❏ c. dissolves.

2. The three states of matter are solid, liquid, and
   - ❏ a. fire.
   - ❏ b. ice.
   - ❏ c. gas.

3. Water freezes at
   - ❏ a. 32 degrees Celsius.
   - ❏ b. 0 degrees Celsius.
   - ❏ c. 100 degrees Celsius.

4. The mathematician who first understood buoyancy was
   - ❏ a. Aristotle.
   - ❏ b. Pythagoras.
   - ❏ c. Archimedes.

5. Water pressure increases with the
   - ❏ a. depth of the water.
   - ❏ b. freshness of the water.
   - ❏ c. color of the water.

Understanding Ideas

6. You could assume that if humans tried to live on Mars,
   - ❏ a. they would find plenty of water on the planet.
   - ❏ b. enough water could be obtained from rain.
   - ❏ c. they would need to find a way to ensure a water supply.

7. At which depth of water would you expect the water pressure to be greatest?
   - ❏ a. 10 feet
   - ❏ b. 50 feet
   - ❏ c. 25 feet

8. If an object is buoyant, you can assume that the water is
   - ❏ a. pushing the object up.
   - ❏ b. pulling the object down.
   - ❏ c. having no effect.

9. In general, it is more likely that
   - ❏ a. the bottom of an ocean has greater water pressure than the bottom of a lake.
   - ❏ b. the bottom of a lake has greater water pressure than the bottom of an ocean.
   - ❏ c. the bottoms of oceans and lakes have equal water pressure.

10. Which of the following can you conclude from the article?
    - ❏ a. An object that is denser than water will float.
    - ❏ b. Buoyancy does not occur in freshwater.
    - ❏ c. An object that is denser than water will not float.

You can imagine how hard it is for plants to grow along muddy, saltwater shores. First, it is difficult for plants to grow in mud without falling over. Second, plants that grow on land require freshwater; not salt water. But mangrove trees have succeeded where other plants have failed.

Mangroves have developed specialized ways of coping with their harsh, muddy environment. Mangrove roots are shallow. They grow into a mass that "floats" in mud, somewhat like a raft. The roots are covered with a bark that resists the acids that form in the mud. Some species have "breathing roots," which grow straight out of the mud. Most mangrove species get rid of the salt in salt water by forcing it out through their leaves.

There are 34 species of mangrove trees. Mangroves grow along the coasts of Florida as well as in other tropical areas around the world. They cannot tolerate cold climates.

The mangrove trees create a rich habitat for many creatures. Their root systems provide a perfect nursery for baby fish. Mangroves also create a good roosting base for pelicans and ospreys. Snakes, proboscis monkeys, otters, and bats are just some of the animals that call the mangrove trees their home.

1. **Recognizing Words in Context**

   Find the word *specialized* in the passage. One definition below is closest to the meaning of that word. One definition has the opposite or nearly opposite meaning. The remaining definition has a completely different meaning. Label the definitions C for *closest,* O for *opposite or nearly opposite,* and D for *different.*

   _____ a. designed for general use

   _____ b. designed for a special purpose

   _____ c. designed for plants

2. **Distinguishing Fact from Opinion**

   Two of the statements below present *facts,* which can be proved correct. The other statement is an *opinion,* which expresses someone's thoughts or beliefs. Label the statements F for *fact* and O for *opinion.*

   _____ a. Mangrove trees are home to a variety of creatures.

   _____ b. Everyone seems to enjoy mangrove trees.

   _____ c. Mangrove trees have adapted to their harsh environment.

3. Keeping Events in Order

Label the statements below 1, 2, and 3 to show the order in which the events happen.

_____ a. A plant tries to grow on a saltwater shore.

_____ b. Salt water flows into the plant and kills it.

_____ c. The tide come in and washes over the plant.

4. Making Correct Inferences

Two of the statements below are correct *inferences,* or reasonable guesses. They are based on information in the passage. The other statement is an incorrect, or faulty, inference. Label the statements C for *correct* inference and F for *faulty* inference.

_____ a. Mangrove roots are a place where baby fish are safe from predators.

_____ b. Mangroves have a raft of roots that help the tree stand in the mud.

_____ c. All species of mangrove trees have adapted in the same way.

5. Understanding Main Ideas

One of the statements below expresses the main idea of the passage. One statement is too general, or too broad. The other explains only part of the passage; it is too narrow. Label the statements M for *main idea,* B for *too broad, and* N for *too narrow.*

_____ a. Mangrove trees have adapted to a harsh environment.

_____ b. Bats and monkeys live in mangrove trees.

_____ c. Seashores have a unique environment.

Correct Answers, Part A _____

Correct Answers, Part B _____

Total Correct Answers _____

Printing has changed tremendously during the past century. Think how easy it is to print a report for school from your computer. And it takes only a few seconds to make a color copy of a picture.

Imagine if you were doing a report and you had to carve each letter out of a block of wood. Think how long it would take to print even a brief report that way! Yet, back in the sixth century A.D., wood-block printing was considered as revolutionary as wireless faxes are today.

The Chinese were the first to use wood-block printing. Even though it took a lot of time, it was much faster than writing each copy. The first step in wood-block printing was to write the text in ink on fine paper. Then the side of the paper with the writing was pressed against the surface of a wooden block that had been coated with rice paste. The paste pulled off some of the ink. Then the paper was removed from the block. Next, an engraver cut away the parts of the wood that had no ink. This made the writing stand out. To make a print, a worker would brush ink on the wood block and press the paper against the wood.

By the 1200s, people in Korea began to print with metal blocks, which lasted longer than wooden blocks. In the mid-1400s, Johannes Gutenberg invented the printing press. This was truly a revolution in printing. In 1455, Gutenberg produced multiple copies of the Bible. This Gutenberg Bible is considered to be the first substantial publication of a book. It took Gutenberg two years to complete the printing.

Several important advances in printing were made in the late 19th century and the 20th century. The typewriter was the first tool for personal, in-home printing. This machine was perfected in 1873. Offset printing, in which text is transferred from a metal-plated cylinder to a rubber-coated cylinder and then onto paper, was invented in 1904. Photocopiers began to be widely used in the 1950s.

Fast-forward to today—to digital printing and the wonders of the Internet for written communication. Written information can be sent directly from one computer to another. Voice-activation programs make it possible for computers to type out words as they are spoken. Just as Gutenberg never imagined the home computer, we can only wonder what machines will be invented in the future.

Reading Time _____

Recalling Facts

1. The first people to use wood-block printing were the
   - ❑ a. Chinese.
   - ❑ b. Japanese.
   - ❑ c. Koreans.

2. The first substantial publication was
   - ❑ a. Aesop's Fables.
   - ❑ b. the Gutenberg Bible.
   - ❑ c. Grimm's Fairy Tales.

3. In wood-block printing, an engraver was needed to
   - ❑ a. make sure the letters were precise.
   - ❑ b. carve away the inked letters on the block.
   - ❑ c. oversee the final printing job.

4. The next advancement in printing after wood-block printing was
   - ❑ a. the typewriter.
   - ❑ b. typesetting.
   - ❑ c. metal-block printing.

5. The first printing press was invented by
   - ❑ a. Gutenberg.
   - ❑ b. Franklin.
   - ❑ c. Galileo.

Understanding Ideas

6. With the creation of the printing press, the availability of printed materials most likely
   - ❑ a. decreased.
   - ❑ b. increased.
   - ❑ c. stayed about the same.

7. Which of the following can you conclude from the article?
   - ❑ a. Metal blocks were more durable than wooden blocks.
   - ❑ b. Metal blocks were more difficult to use than wooden blocks.
   - ❑ c. Wood-block printing was a fast process.

8. If you were able to print in your home in the late 19th century, you probably had a
   - ❑ a. typewriter.
   - ❑ b. personal computer.
   - ❑ c. wood-block printer.

9. Advances in printing have
   - ❑ a. dramatically affected our world today.
   - ❑ b. had no effect on our world.
   - ❑ c. made us less productive at work.

10. You can conclude from the article that
    - ❑ a. new ways of printing are always being developed.
    - ❑ b. printing will not change much in the future.
    - ❑ c. printing hasn't changed since the printing press.

Hieroglyphs Uncovered

Can you remember drawing pictures of your family members or friends when you were a young child? Maybe you drew only "stick people," but they represented real people to you. Your pictures were like hieroglyphs. Hieroglyphs are Egyptian picture writing.

For a long time, people were not able to read Egyptian hieroglyphs. In 1799, archaeologists uncovered the Rosetta stone during a dig at Rashid in northern Egypt. This stone contained three specific kinds of writing: Egyptian hieroglyphs, an earlier Egyptian script called demotic script, and Greek. Because scholars could read the Greek, they could read some of the Egyptian demotic script. This led to a breakthrough. Scholars determined that hieroglyphs were based on phonetic signs. This means that the hieroglyphs were based on patterns and sounds of human speech.

There are three types of hieroglyphs. Alphabetic hieroglyphs represent a letter or sound. Syllabic hieroglyphs represent sounds produced by a group of letters, such as *sh*. Determinative hieroglyphs relate to an object or idea, such as *water* or *life*.

Hieroglyphs may be written either horizontally or in columns. They can be read left-to-right or right-to-left. To read a group of hieroglyphs, you must find the face characters. If they face right, read right-to-left. If they face left, read left-to-right. Learning to read hieroglyphs helped scholars to gain a much better understanding of the history of ancient Egypt.

1. **Recognizing Words in Context**

   Find the word *specific* in the passage. One definition below is closest to the meaning of that word. One definition has the opposite or nearly opposite meaning. The remaining definition has a completely different meaning. Label the definitions C for *closest*, O for *opposite or nearly opposite*, and D for *different*.

   _____ a. beautiful

   _____ b. unclear

   _____ c. definite

2. **Distinguishing Fact from Opinion**

   Two of the statements below present *facts*, which can be proved correct. The other statement is an *opinion*, which expresses someone's thoughts or beliefs. Label the statements F for *fact* and O for *opinion*.

   _____ a. The Rosetta stone was the key to understanding Egyptian hieroglyphs.

   _____ b. Egyptian hieroglyphs may be read either left-to-right or right-to-left.

   _____ c. Egyptian hieroglyphs are interesting to study.

3. Keeping Events in Order

Label the statements below 1, 2, and 3 to show the order in which the events happened.

_____ a. Egyptians invented hieroglyphs.

_____ b. Archaeologists discovered the Rosetta stone.

_____ c. Scholars learned Egyptian hieroglyphs were based on phonetic sounds.

4. Making Correct Inferences

Two of the statements below are correct *inferences,* or reasonable guesses. They are based on information in the passage. The other statement is an incorrect, or faulty, inference. Label the statements C for *correct* inference and F for *faulty* inference.

_____ a. Ancient Egyptians had a complex form of written communication.

_____ b. Hieroglyphs are a poor form of communication.

_____ c. Understanding hieroglyphs can help us understand the culture of ancient Egypt.

5. Understanding Main Ideas

One of the statements below expresses the main idea of the passage. One statement is too general, or too broad. The other explains only part of the passage; it is too narrow. Label the statements M for *main idea,* B for *too broad,* and N for *too narrow.*

_____ a. Hieroglyphs are a complex form of writing.

_____ b. Ancient Egypt was an advanced civilization.

_____ c. The Rosetta stone contains three types of writing.

Correct Answers, Part A _____

Correct Answers, Part B _____

Total Correct Answers _____

The world is full of new things to discover. Through a process of experimenting and documenting, we can find out how different parts of the natural world work. This is called the scientific process, or scientific method. The scientific process is a standardized method of finding out about things we don't understand. Scientists and explorers all over the world use the same method for forming theories and proving their findings. Using the same method helps scientists work together more effectively.

The scientific process can be broken down into steps. The first step is to pose a question about something you have observed in the natural world. The wording you use for the question is very important. A question must be objective—it can't deal with values or feelings.

After you establish a question, create a hypothesis. A hypothesis is simply a statement of what you expect to happen during an experiment. Suppose your question is "What will happen to seeds if I change the temperature they are kept at before I plant them?" Your hypothesis might be "The higher the temperature at which I keep the seeds, the quicker I expect them to sprout."

The next step is to write a procedure for your experiment. This will include all the steps needed to carry out the experiment. The procedure must have only one variable. This means you can change only one of the conditions in the experiment. In the seed-sprouting experiment, your variable might be the temperature. You would need to make sure that all the other factors are the same, including the type and size of seed and the amount of light and water you give the seeds after they are planted.

Then conduct your experiment. After you complete your experiment, record your results—the specific information you gathered during the experiment. Include measurements when you record your results. For example, you shouldn't say the sprouts were "bigger," because *bigger* is a subjective word. You should say something such as "Sprout A grew 1 centimeter on day 2." After you record your results, draw a conclusion. The conclusion is your understanding of what the data mean. Sometimes your conclusion will prove your hypothesis to be wrong. That's OK! You will still have learned something on your path of discovery. You should keep trying with different hypotheses until you find one that you can prove to be true.

Reading Time _____

Recalling Facts

1. The scientific process is also called the
   - ❏ a. record keeping method.
   - ❏ b. experimentation method.
   - ❏ c. scientific method.

2. The first step in the scientific process is
   - ❏ a. posing a question.
   - ❏ b. recording data.
   - ❏ c. performing an experiment.

3. The statement that explains what you hope to learn from your experiment is called a
   - ❏ a. conclusion.
   - ❏ b. hypothesis.
   - ❏ c. query.

4. An experiment should have only one
   - ❏ a. variable.
   - ❏ b. control group.
   - ❏ c. scientist.

5. Your understanding of the data is your
   - ❏ a. hypothesis.
   - ❏ b. opinion.
   - ❏ c. conclusion.

Understanding Ideas

6. Which of the following is a good scientific question?
   - ❏ a. Are ants hard workers?
   - ❏ b. Would the black widow spider make a good pet?
   - ❏ c. If I lower the temperature of my aquarium two degrees, what will happen to the female guppy?

7. Which of the following cannot be concluded from the article?
   - ❏ a. Experiments always prove the hypothesis to be correct.
   - ❏ b. If your hypothesis is not correct, you have still learned something.
   - ❏ c. A conclusion is the analysis of the data.

8. The most likely reason that only one condition in an experiment can be changed is because more than one change would affect the
   - ❏ a. time frame.
   - ❏ b. outcome.
   - ❏ c. cost.

9. One advantage of the scientific method is that
   - ❏ a. all labs would have the same equipment.
   - ❏ b. there is a universal standard for understanding findings.
   - ❏ c. no one is able to copy another person's work.

10. If the results of an experiment are not recorded in detail, then the
    - ❏ a. conclusion may not be accurate.
    - ❏ b. question was not valid.
    - ❏ c. hypothesis was wrong.

One of the first questions young children ask is "Why?" It's human nature to want to find out why things are the way they are. You can find out "why" by turning the question into a hypothesis for an experiment.

For example, suppose you have been trying to grow tomato plants, but insects keep destroying them. Someone tells you that putting large strips of colored fabric around the plants will keep insects away. Your question might be "Do certain colors of fabric repel insects?" Then you'd begin your experiment. The first step would be to place different-colored strips of fabric around all of the plants except one. Then, at regular intervals, you would observe and record the type of insects found on each plant. You would also record the number of insects and note whether the plant had any insect damage.

This experiment may prove that the answer to your question is "No, different-colored fabric strips do not repel insects." Or you may find that the answer is "Yes, certain insects are repelled by blue cloth, but not yellow cloth." Or you may have discovered something else. Whatever your findings, you are well on your way to understanding how you can use scientific thinking to solve a problem in your own life.

1. Recognizing Words in Context

Find the word *repel* in the passage. One definition below is closest to the meaning of that word. One definition has the opposite or nearly opposite meaning. The remaining definition has a completely different meaning. Label the definitions C for *closest,* O for *opposite or nearly opposite,* and D for *different.*

_____ a. involve

_____ b. attract

_____ c. drive away

2. Distinguishing Fact from Opinion

Two of the statements below present *facts,* which can be proved correct. The other statement is an *opinion,* which expresses someone's thoughts or beliefs. Label the statements F for *fact* and O for *opinion.*

_____ a. Growing tomatoes is a worthwhile activity.

_____ b. Creating a hypothesis can help you begin to understand the world.

_____ c. An experiment may either prove or disprove the hypothesis.

3. Keeping Events in Order

Label the statements below 1, 2, and 3 to show the order in which the events happen.

_____ a. You place fabric strips around most of the plants.

_____ b. You observe whether insects have been attracted to the fabric.

_____ c. Insects have been destroying your tomato plants.

4. Making Correct Inferences

Two of the statements below are correct *inferences*, or reasonable guesses. They are based on information in the passage. The other statement is an incorrect, or faulty, inference. Label the statements C for *correct* inference and F for *faulty* inference.

_____ a. It might be possible to repel insects with colored fabric.

_____ b. All insects are repelled by the same color fabric.

_____ c. Experiments can tell us many things about the natural world.

5. Understanding Main Ideas

One of the statements below expresses the main idea of the passage. One statement is too general, or too broad. The other explains only part of the passage; it is too narrow. Label the statements M for *main idea*, B for *too broad*, and N for *too narrow*.

_____ a. Some tomato plants were wrapped with blue fabric.

_____ b. Scientists conduct experiments.

_____ c. The scientific process can help answer questions you have about nature.

Correct Answers, Part A _____

Correct Answers, Part B _____

Total Correct Answers _____

Some days it's just hard to get out of bed in the morning. Imagine if you lived in the wild, where you have to search for food constantly, endure frequent bad weather, and avoid being eaten. This is what wild animals have to deal with when they wake up in the morning. They don't have the luxury of sleeping in.

Life in the natural world is dangerous and unpredictable. Animals compete for survival not only with other species but also with their own species. To survive from day to day, animals have developed a number of interesting and effective defense systems.

Camouflage is a very effective method of protection. Animals with camouflage blend in with their natural surroundings. Lizards, insects, and some birds are among the animals that use camouflage. An insect called the walking stick looks like a twig from a tree.

Odor can be a very powerful defense. When you think of "stinky" animals, you may think of the skunk first. However, cockroaches, bedbugs, earwigs, foxes, mink, snakes, and weasels also use scent glands to deter their predators.

Poison is one of the most feared defenses. Some spiders and snakes have poisonous bites. The inland taipan snake of Australia is so poisonous that the venom from just one bite can kill up to 100 people. There are also species of poisonous toads and moths. Some fish, such as the stonefish and the scorpion fish, have poisonous spines.

You might not think that spitting could help an animal to defend itself very well, but many animals find it quite effective. Spitting can be used to get food or to injure a predator. The archerfish swims to the surface of the water and spits at insects, stunning the insects and causing them to fall into the water, where the fish eats them. The spitting cobra spits poisonous venom into the eyes of its enemies and prey.

Horns, antlers, and tusks are easily visible methods of defense. Goats, sheep, and water buffalo are among the animals that have horns. Elk, moose, and other members of the deer family have antlers. Walruses, elephants, and wild boars are some of the animals that have tusks.

If you go camping or hiking in the wild, make sure you are aware of any dangerous animals that live in the area. Many of these animals will not bother you unless you bother them.

Reading Time _____

Recalling Facts

1. One of the biggest challenges facing animals in the wild is
   - ❑ a. exercising.
   - ❑ b. sleeping.
   - ❑ c. surviving.

2. Animals need to find ways to protect themselves because life can be
   - ❑ a. exciting.
   - ❑ b. dangerous.
   - ❑ c. fun.

3. Odor is a powerful defense for the
   - ❑ a. cockroach.
   - ❑ b. turtle.
   - ❑ c. eagle.

4. An animal with camouflage is able to
   - ❑ a. find food faster.
   - ❑ b. stand out from its surroundings.
   - ❑ c. blend in with its surroundings.

5. The stonefish has poisonous
   - ❑ a. scales.
   - ❑ b. spines.
   - ❑ c. fins.

Understanding Ideas

6. Animals have developed defenses that
   - ❑ a. help them to survive.
   - ❑ b. make it more difficult for them to survive.
   - ❑ c. compete with other animals.

7. When trapped, a wild boar would most likely
   - ❑ a. blend in with its surroundings.
   - ❑ b. give a poisonous bite.
   - ❑ c. attack with its tusks.

8. A skunk would most likely spray you if you
   - ❑ a. startled and scared it.
   - ❑ b. went out of your way to avoid it.
   - ❑ c. drove a car past it.

9. Over time, animals have developed their defense systems based largely on the basis of
   - ❑ a. human involvement.
   - ❑ b. environmental conditions.
   - ❑ c. how long they live.

10. The more effective an animal's defense system is, the more likely the animal is able to
    - ❑ a. kill other species.
    - ❑ b. live a longer life.
    - ❑ c. move from region to region.

Skunks are one of the most misunderstood animals on the planet. Because skunks often live near humans and emit such strong musky odors, we tend to be afraid of them. Skunks are omnivores, which means they eat both plants and animals. This makes them both helpful and annoying to humans. They help to reduce the insect and rodent population, but they also damage crops and eat hens' eggs and pet food.

Skunks are solitary creatures that tend to avoid contact with others. Sometimes they make their homes under houses. This process is called denning. They also like to live in open irrigation pipes, junked cars, and dry brush piles. They are best known for their odor defense system. If a skunk has ever sprayed you, you know how hard it is to get rid of the odor. If you startle a skunk, it is likely to turn its scent glands on you and spray. It can spray up to 15 feet away.

When a skunk is frightened, it will stamp its feet while raising its tail before releasing the musk from its scent glands. If you get sprayed, you can neutralize the odor with a solution containing neutroleum alpha. You can soak your clothes in tomato juice or in a diluted solution of vinegar or household ammonia. If you encounter a skunk, move slowly away from it. If you avoid the skunk, chances are the skunk will avoid spraying you!

1. **Recognizing Words in Context**

   Find the word *solitary* in the passage. One definition below is closest to the meaning of that word. One definition has the opposite or nearly opposite meaning. The remaining definition has a completely different meaning. Label the definitions C for *closest,* O for *opposite or nearly opposite,* and D for *different.*

   _____ a. intelligent

   _____ b. sociable

   _____ c. lone

2. **Distinguishing Fact from Opinion**

   Two of the statements below present *facts,* which can be proved correct. The other statement is an *opinion,* which expresses someone's thoughts or beliefs. Label the statements F for *fact* and O for *opinion.*

   _____ a. Skunks eat plants and animals.

   _____ b. Skunks are unpleasant.

   _____ c. Skunks can spray up to 15 feet.

3. **Keeping Events in Order**

Label the statements below 1, 2, and 3 to show the order in which the events happen.

_____ a. The skunk stamps its feet.

_____ b. Someone frightens a skunk.

_____ c. The skunk sprays its foul-smelling musk.

4. **Making Correct Inferences**

Two of the statements below are correct *inferences,* or reasonable guesses. They are based on information in the passage. The other statement is an incorrect, or faulty, inference. Label the statements C for *correct* inference and F for *faulty* inference.

_____ a. Skunks are aggressive and often attack humans.

_____ b. If you stay out of a skunk's way, it will probably stay out of yours.

_____ c. An old barn is the type of place where skunks would like to dig dens.

5. **Understanding Main Ideas**

One of the statements below expresses the main idea of the passage. One statement is too general, or too broad. The other explains only part of the passage; it is too narrow. Label the statements M for *main idea,* B for *too broad,* and N for *too narrow.*

_____ a. Some animals are hard to like.

_____ b. Skunks can spray their scent up to 15 feet.

_____ c. Skunks are misunderstood animals.

Correct Answers, Part A _____

Correct Answers, Part B _____

Total Correct Answers _____

How the Heart Works

The heart beats the rhythm to your life. It speeds up when you're excited. It slows down when you're relaxed. Each day, the average person's heart beats about 100,000 times. In a 70-year life, that's more than 2.5 billion beats!

Your heart beats when it expands and contracts. The heartbeat is controlled by an electrical charge. This charge is created by the sinus node, a small mass of specialized muscle fibers located in the right side of the heart.

The heart is a very strong muscle, slightly larger than a fist. Its job is to constantly pump blood through the circulatory system. The circulatory system consists of the heart, the lungs, and a network of tubes that extends throughout the body. These tubes include arteries, veins, and tiny blood vessels called capillaries.

The blood that travels through arteries carries oxygen to the body. The blood that travels through veins removes carbon dioxide. Capillaries connect arteries with veins. The main artery of the circulatory system is the aorta. The aorta carries blood to all the branch arteries in the body except the lungs. About 5 liters (5.3 quarts) of blood circulate through the body.

The heart has four chambers. The upper two chambers are called the right atrium and the left atrium. The lower two chambers are called the right ventricle and the left ventricle. A wall of muscle called a septum separates the right and left sides.

Valves connect all the chambers. They allow the blood to pass through the heart in only one direction. The heart has four valves, two on each side of the heart. The valves open and close to let blood flow properly.

The process of the heart's pumping blood through the body is called the cardiac cycle. During the cycle, the right atrium receives blood from all the organs except the lungs. The blood is received through two large veins called the superior vena cava and the inferior vena cava. The right atrium passes blood to the right ventricle. The right ventricle pumps the blood through the pulmonary artery. The pulmonary artery takes the blood to the lungs, where the blood picks up oxygen. Oxygen-rich blood is then returned to the left atrium through the pulmonary veins. That blood goes from the left atrium into the left ventricle, where it is pumped out to the rest of the body through the aorta. An entire cycle takes about 60 seconds.

Reading Time _____

Recalling Facts

1. How many liters of blood does the body have?
   - ❏ a. five
   - ❏ b. four
   - ❏ c. fifteen

2. The expanding and contracting of the heart is called a
   - ❏ a. breath.
   - ❏ b. heartbeat.
   - ❏ c. muscle.

3. The sinus node creates
   - ❏ a. oxygen-rich blood.
   - ❏ b. an electrical charge.
   - ❏ c. a wall of muscle.

4. One of the lower chambers of the heart is the
   - ❏ a. right aorta.
   - ❏ b. vena cava.
   - ❏ c. left ventricle.

5. Carbon dioxide is removed from the body by the
   - ❏ a. arteries.
   - ❏ b. valves.
   - ❏ c. veins.

Understanding Ideas

6. From the article you can assume that the heart is
   - ❏ a. a simple muscle.
   - ❏ b. an inefficient muscle.
   - ❏ c. a specialized muscle.

7. If you are taking a ride on a roller coaster, it is most likely that your heartbeat will
   - ❏ a. speed up.
   - ❏ b. slow down.
   - ❏ c. stay the same.

8. The primary function of the heart is to
   - ❏ a. regulate brain waves.
   - ❏ b. aid in temperature control.
   - ❏ c. pump blood through the circulatory system.

9. You can conclude from the article that in a healthy heart, the cardiac cycle is usually
   - ❏ a. irregular.
   - ❏ b. regular.
   - ❏ c. longer than three minutes.

10. Which organs are part of the circulatory system?
    - ❏ a. the heart and the kidney
    - ❏ b. the liver and the lungs
    - ❏ c. the lungs and the heart

A healthy heart is the key to a healthy body. Keeping the heart fit now can help prevent problems, such as heart disease, high blood pressure, and stroke. One of the best ways to keep the heart healthy is to get regular aerobic exercise.

Aerobic means "with air." When you are doing an aerobic exercise, you should use the same group of large muscles for at least 15 minutes. During that time, you should maintain 60 to 80 percent of your maximum heart rate. You should be able to carry on a short conversation while exercising. Some examples of aerobic exercise are swimming, bicycling, walking, and jogging.

There are many benefits to regular aerobic exercise. Your heart benefits because your lungs will be able to process more air with less effort. This means your heart can pump more blood with fewer beats. At the same time, aerobic exercise can increase the blood supply sent to your muscles. Exercising regularly—at least three times per week—increases the efficiency of your circulatory system. Other benefits of aerobic exercise include reduced stress, extra energy, and increased muscle tone.

Before you begin an exercise routine, check with your doctor. Begin slowly and don't overdo it. Remember, keep breathing and have fun! You are taking the first step toward a long and healthy life.

1. **Recognizing Words in Context**
   Find the word *efficiency* in the passage. One definition below is closest to the meaning of that word. One definition has the opposite or nearly opposite meaning. The remaining definition has a completely different meaning. Label the definitions C for *closest*, O for *opposite or nearly opposite*, and D for *different*.

   _____ a. effectiveness

   _____ b. wastefulness

   _____ c. brightness

2. **Distinguishing Fact from Opinion**
   Two of the statements below present *facts*, which can be proved correct. The other statement is an *opinion*, which expresses someone's thoughts or beliefs. Label the statements F for *fact* and O for *opinion*.

   _____ a. Hiking is the best form of aerobic exercise.

   _____ b. *Aerobic* means "with air."

   _____ c. Bicycling is one type of aerobic exercise.

3. Keeping Events in Order

Label the statements below 1, 2, and 3 to show the order in which the events would happen.

_____ a. Your lungs process air with less effort.

_____ b. You begin an exercise routine.

_____ c. Even a small amount of work leaves you short of breath.

4. Making Correct Inferences

Two of the statements below are correct *inferences*, or reasonable guesses. They are based on information in the passage. The other statement is an incorrect, or faulty, inference. Label the statements C for *correct* inference and F for *faulty* inference.

_____ a. Regular exercise can help reduce heart disease.

_____ b. If you begin exercising, you'll increase muscle tone.

_____ c. If you swim every day, you will never have a heart attack.

5. Understanding Main Ideas

One of the statements below expresses the main idea of the passage. One statement is too general, or too broad. The other explains only part of the passage; it is too narrow. Label the statements M for *main idea*, B for *too broad*, and N for *too narrow*.

_____ a. Regular aerobic exercise is beneficial to the body.

_____ b. Jogging is an effective form of aerobic exercise.

_____ c. It's important that the heart be kept healthy.

Correct Answers, Part A _____

Correct Answers, Part B _____

Total Correct Answers _____

Types of Volcanoes

Volcanoes are a crucial part of Earth's geology. The eruption of a volcano is one of the ways Earth releases its internal pressures. These pressures force molten rock, called magma, upward from Earth's interior, creating a volcano. There are three main types of volcanoes. These types are based on the shape of the volcano and the type of material that comes out of the ground. The three types of volcanoes are scoria cone volcanoes, shield volcanoes, and stratovolcanoes.

Scoria cone volcanoes are the smallest and most common volcanoes. They are often less than 300 meters (1,000 feet) high. These volcanoes have steep slopes and large craters at the summit. They are often symmetrical. Scoria cone volcanoes were formed by eruptions that produced piles of tephra. Tephra consists of pieces of basalt rock, both tiny and large, that are blown out of Earth during a volcanic eruption. Most scoria cone volcanoes erupt once, although some, such as Cerro Negro in Nicaragua, erupt more often.

Shield volcanoes have a broad, gently sloped shape. The diameters of their bases can vary from 3 to 60 kilometers (2 to 35 miles). Mauna Loa in Hawaii is an example of a shield volcano. Shield volcanoes are often 20 times wider than they are tall. These volcanoes are created by large flows of very fluid lava. Sometimes the lava stops flowing and then starts again, resulting in many layers of rock

Stratovolcanoes are a combination of scoria cone volcanoes and shield volcanoes. Stratovolcanoes contain both hardened lava and tephra. Some of the most scenic volcanoes are stratovolcanoes. They often slope gently at the bottom and become steep toward the top, with a small crater at the summit. Although this type of volcano rarely erupts, the results are deadly when it does. The eruptions, called plinian eruptions, are composed of hot volcanic fragments and toxic gases. The lava may rush down the slopes at great speeds. Mount Saint Helens in Washington, a stratovolcano, erupted violently in 1980.

Scientists call a volcano active if it shows signs of erupting in the near future. If a volcano does not show signs of erupting, it is known as a dormant volcano. Even though volcanic eruptions can be dangerous, volcanoes are part of the natural cycle of life on Earth. Each time a volcano erupts, pressure is released from Earth's core. This helps to keep our planet stable.

Reading Time _____

Recalling Facts

1. Tephra consists of
   - ❏ a. pieces of basalt.
   - ❏ b. lava.
   - ❏ c. toxic gases.

2. An example of a stratovolcano is
   - ❏ a. Cerro Negro.
   - ❏ b. Mauna Loa.
   - ❏ c. Mount Saint Helens.

3. The type of volcano known for its rare but deadly eruptions is the
   - ❏ a. shield volcano.
   - ❏ b. stratovolcano.
   - ❏ c. scoria cone volcano.

4. Scoria cone volcanoes are rarely more than
   - ❏ a. 300 meters high.
   - ❏ b. 100 meters high.
   - ❏ c. 200 feet high.

5. The most common type of volcano is the
   - ❏ a. stratovolcano.
   - ❏ b. shield volcano.
   - ❏ c. scoria cone volcano.

Understanding Ideas

6. If you see a volcano that has a gently sloping shape, it is most likely a
   - ❏ a. shield volcano.
   - ❏ b. stratovolcano.
   - ❏ c. scoria cone volcano.

7. You can conclude from the article that volcanoes
   - ❏ a. are the most common landform on Earth.
   - ❏ b. erupt continuously.
   - ❏ c. help to shape the land.

8. A volcanic eruption is likely when
   - ❏ a. there is a buildup of internal pressure beneath Earth's crust.
   - ❏ b. there is a total lunar eclipse.
   - ❏ c. the seasons change.

9. From this article, you can conclude that volcanoes are
   - ❏ a. near oceans or major rivers.
   - ❏ b. approximately the same height.
   - ❏ c. found in various parts of the world.

10. If a volcano is active, you can assume
   - ❏ a. it will never erupt.
   - ❏ b. it may erupt one day.
   - ❏ c. it is a very large mountain.

13   B   Mount Rainier

In 1792, Captain George Vancouver sailed into Puget Sound in what is now Washington State. He saw a huge mountain that he named Mount Rainier in honor of his friend, Peter Rainier. He didn't know he was looking at an active volcano. Mount Rainier stands about 4,400 meters (14,400 feet) above sea level. People in the Seattle area call it The Mountain. Its base covers an area of about 260 square kilometers (100 square miles).

Mount Rainier is a stratovolcano. It first erupted about 500,000 years ago. Nearly 6,000 years ago, there were violent steam explosions on the mountain. This caused one of the largest mudflows in history. Large eruptions have occurred as recently as 1,000 years ago. The volcano's most striking features are vast glaciers. They cover 94 square kilometers (36 square miles) of the mountain's surface.

Scientists expect that Mount Rainier may erupt again within the next 300 years, but not in the near future. There are occasional small explosions of steam on its upper slopes. The top crater has many steam vents as well as hot rocks. An eruption could cause dangerous mudflows and floods. Flying tephra is another possible danger.

Though the volcano is dormant now, no one knows exactly what the future holds for Mount Rainier.

1. Recognizing Words in Context

Find the word *striking* in the passage. One definition below is closest to the meaning of that word. One definition has the opposite or nearly opposite meaning. The remaining definition has a completely different meaning. Label the definitions C for *closest,* O for *opposite or nearly opposite,* and D for *different.*

_____ a. invisible

_____ b. violent

_____ c. noticeable

2. Distinguishing Fact from Opinion

Two of the statements below present *facts,* which can be proved correct. The other statement is an *opinion,* which expresses someone's thoughts or beliefs. Label the statements F for *fact* and O for *opinion.*

_____ a. Mount Rainier is the most beautiful volcano.

_____ b. Mount Rainier is a dormant volcano.

_____ c. There are steam explosions on Mount Rainier's upper slopes.

3. Keeping Events in Order

Label the statements below 1, 2, and 3 to show the order in which the events happened.

_____ a. Steam explosions erupted from Mount Rainier.

_____ b. One of the largest mud-flows in history occurred.

_____ c. A large quantity of snow melted.

4. Making Correct Inferences

Two of the statements below are correct *inferences*, or reasonable guesses. They are based on information in the passage. The other statement is an incorrect, or faulty, inference. Label the statements C for *correct* inference and F for *faulty* inference.

_____ a. If Mount Rainier erupts, the damage could be severe.

_____ b. Once a volcano erupts, it never erupts again.

_____ c. A dormant volcano may still erupt one day.

5. Understanding Main Ideas

One of the statements below expresses the main idea of the passage. One statement is too general, or too broad. The other explains only part of the passage; it is too narrow. Label the statements M for *main idea,* B for *too broad,* and N for *too narrow.*

_____ a. Volcanic eruptions can have devastating effects.

_____ b. Mount Rainier has an interesting history and an unpredictable future.

_____ c. Mount Rainier was named for Peter Rainier.

Correct Answers, Part A _____

Correct Answers, Part B _____

Total Correct Answers _____

The Prairie Ecosystem

A prairie is a type of grassland. Prairies are unique because they consist of a complete interdependent ecosystem. This means that all species of plants and animals in a prairie region depend on one another for survival. The members of a prairie ecosystem include grasses, flowering plants, animals, soil, sand, and fire.

You may look at a prairie and think there's nothing there but grass, but that's not the case at all. Most of the prairie's living mass is below the ground. Underneath the prairie's surface is a dense mass of roots and bulbs. The roots of the prairie flowers and grasses run deep. Some of them are as deep as 3.5 meters (11 feet) below the ground.

It is important for the roots to run deep because fires are a vital part of the prairie ecosystem. When a fire burns through the prairie, plants with shallow roots cannot survive. Plants that have deep root systems are able to withstand the fires. When fire burns across a prairie, it burns dead material from the tops of plants and returns those nutrients to the soil. Each year there is also some natural decay of plants. All of this adds to the richness of the prairie soil. Prairies have some of the most fertile soil in the United States. This cycle of growth and burning has been going on for thousands of years.

Big bluestem is the plant that gives sections of the prairie the name "tallgrass prairie." Big bluestem has very deep roots, and its stems are often 2 meters (6 feet) tall. The grassy part of the plant grows in bunches. It has short, round stems that are blue or purple. Other prairie grasses include dropseed, wild rye, and switchgrass.

The American bison, or buffalo, is the country's largest land animal. Its home is on the prairies. In 1830, there were an estimated 30 million to 60 million bison in the United States. By 1889, American settlers had reduced the bison population to fewer than 1,000 animals. Through conservation efforts, bison are being reintroduced to the prairies. They are also kept in zoos. The bison population has grown to several hundred thousand today.

Humans have threatened the prairie ecosystem. Through constant farming, building, fire prevention, and ignorance of how the prairie works, the United States has lost much of its natural prairie. Through education and preservation, we can hope to restore some of it.

Reading Time _____

Recalling Facts

1. A prairie is a type of
   - ❏ a. cloud formation.
   - ❏ b. biome.
   - ❏ c. grassland.

2. Some of the roots of prairie grasses are
   - ❏ a. 30 meters deep.
   - ❏ b. 3 meters deep.
   - ❏ c. 3 centimeters deep.

3. The largest land animal in the United States is the
   - ❏ a. American bison.
   - ❏ b. mountain lion.
   - ❏ c. grizzly bear.

4. By 1889, bison herds had been reduced to
   - ❏ a. zero animals.
   - ❏ b. fewer than 1,000 animals.
   - ❏ c. fewer than 100 animals.

5. Prairie soil is
   - ❏ a. rocky.
   - ❏ b. not fertile.
   - ❏ c. fertile.

Understanding Ideas

6. You can conclude from the article that without regular fires the prairie soil would
   - ❏ a. experience no change in its makeup.
   - ❏ b. increase its fertility.
   - ❏ c. lose some of its richness.

7. A word that could be used to describe the prairie ecosystem is
   - ❏ a. simple.
   - ❏ b. independent.
   - ❏ c. complex.

8. The article suggests that
   - ❏ a. all of the prairie's ecosystem is below ground.
   - ❏ b. all of the prairie's ecosystem is above ground.
   - ❏ c. the prairie's ecosystem is both below and above ground.

9. You can assume that the destruction of the American bison had
   - ❏ a. very little effect on the prairie ecosystem.
   - ❏ b. a great effect on the prairie ecosystem.
   - ❏ c. no effect at all on the prairie ecosystem.

10. You could assume that the greatest threat to the prairie ecosystem is
   - ❏ a. humans.
   - ❏ b. fire.
   - ❏ c. drought.

14 B   Prairie Dog Towns

It's early morning in a prairie dog town. One male prairie dog is awake and standing guard over the town. He is on the lookout for danger. If he sees anything, he warns the others with a series of barking-like whistles, called chirking. This sound alerts the rest of the town to trouble.

Prairie dogs are social animals. They live in complex communities called towns or colonies. Prairie dog towns have intricate underground tunnel systems that lead to different kinds of chambers. These chambers usually have beds of dry leaves and grass. Prairie dog towns are divided into neighborhoods, which scientists call wards. Each ward has several coteries. A coterie is a family group made of one male, one to four females, and their young.

Each member of the prairie dog town has a job to do. Some forage for food. Some maintain the burrows. Some care for the young. Prairie dogs eat leafy vegetables, grass, and seeds. Occasionally they eat insects.

Prairie dogs within the same coterie have a special way of greeting each other. They gently touch their front teeth together. Scientists refer to this as "kissing."

Prairie dogs are usually active in the early morning and late afternoon. During the day, if the sun is out, they usually are sleeping underground. If it is overcast or cool, they may stay outside all day.

1. **Recognizing Words in Context**

   Find the word *intricate* in the passage. One definition below is closest to the meaning of that word. One definition has the opposite or nearly opposite meaning. The remaining definition has a completely different meaning. Label the definitions C for *closest,* O for *opposite or nearly opposite,* and D for *different.*

   _____ a. beautiful

   _____ b. simple

   _____ c. complex

2. **Distinguishing Fact from Opinion**

   Two of the statements below present *facts,* which can be proved correct. The other statement is an *opinion,* which expresses someone's thoughts or beliefs. Label the statements F for *fact* and O for *opinion.*

   _____ a. Prairie dogs seem to enjoy their communities.

   _____ b. Prairie dogs live in intricate communities.

   _____ c. Prairie dogs are social animals.

3. Keeping Events in Order

Label the statements below 1, 2, and 3 to show the order in which the events happen.

_____ a. The sentinel watches over the community.

_____ b. The prairie dog community is aware danger is approaching.

_____ c. The sentinel begins to chirk.

4. Making Correct Inferences

Two of the statements below are correct *inferences,* or reasonable guesses. They are based on information in the passage. The other statement is an incorrect, or faulty, inference. Label the statements C for *correct* inference and F for *faulty* inference.

_____ a. The role of sentinel is an important one in the community.

_____ b. Prairie dogs never come out in the middle of the day.

_____ c. If it is overcast, a prairie dog may stay above ground.

5. Understanding Main Ideas

One of the statements below expresses the main idea of the passage. One statement is too general, or too broad. The other explains only part of the passage; it is too narrow. Label the statements M for *main idea,* B for *too broad,* and N for *too narrow.*

_____ a. One job a prairie dog might have is that of a sentinel.

_____ b. Prairie dogs and other rodents live in grasslands.

_____ c. Prairie dogs have a complex, community-based lifestyle.

Correct Answers, Part A _____

Correct Answers, Part B _____

Total Correct Answers _____

Imagine never traveling farther than 15 kilometers (10 miles) from your home. That is what life was often like before the invention of many machines that we take for granted today. The ability to move quickly and efficiently from place to place has shaped our development as humans.

No one knows for sure who invented the wheel. The oldest evidence of a wheel appears on a 5,500-year-old drawing found in Mesopotamia, in what is now Iraq. The discovery of the wheel may have occurred when people observed that fallen trees would roll. The use of the wheel made it possible for people to travel farther to hunt or to trade. A wheelbarrow was one of the first machines built from two simpler machines—the wheel and the lever. This machine allowed people to transport food and other items more easily.

The most significant changes to transportation occurred in the 19th and 20th centuries. In 1830, *The Best Friend of Charleston*—the first steam locomotive to provide regular passenger service in the United States— began its operation. By 1833, the rail system between Charleston and Hamburg, South Carolina, was 216 kilometers (135 miles) long. This was the longest railway in the world. Soon, railroad workers began working west from Omaha and east from San Francisco to build a railroad. By 1869, they met at Promontory Point, Utah. They nailed a golden spike into the tracks. For the first time, rail lines stretched from one end of the country to the other. This made it easier for people to move to the western states.

The next major transportation invention was the internal combustion engine. This type of engine is one that burns a mixture of gasoline and air. The fuel burns inside a cylinder, where a piston is forced down. This force provides the power to make wheels roll. Nikolaus Otto invented the first successful internal combustion engine in 1876. This invention led to the development of the automobile.

A car is a "kit" made up of many machines. The engine provides power. The transmission carries the power through gears and into the axles and tires. The steering system allows the driver to control the direction the car moves in. The braking system causes the car to stop moving. Of course, there are many other machines working within a car.

We now have airplanes and space shuttles to help us get from place to place. What will this century bring?

Reading Time _____

Recalling Facts

1. The first evidence of a wheel was found in
   - ❑ a. Mesopotamia.
   - ❑ b. India.
   - ❑ c. Rome.

2. The wheelbarrow was built using a wheel and a
   - ❑ a. motor.
   - ❑ b. lever.
   - ❑ c. pulley.

3. The internal combustion engine led to the development of the
   - ❑ a. wheelbarrow.
   - ❑ b. space shuttle.
   - ❑ c. automobile.

4. The rail system between Charleston and Hamburg, South Carolina, was
   - ❑ a. 250 km long.
   - ❑ b. 216 km long.
   - ❑ c. 316 km long.

5. The first successful internal combustion engine was invented by
   - ❑ a. John Dunlop.
   - ❑ b. Benjamin Franklin.
   - ❑ c. Nikolaus Otto.

Understanding Ideas

6. An engine that burns a mixture of gasoline and air in a cylinder is called
   - ❑ a. an internal combustion engine.
   - ❑ b. a steam engine.
   - ❑ c. an automatic transmission.

7. The wheel may have been invented because primitive people had
   - ❑ a. watched a solar eclipse.
   - ❑ b. noticed that fallen trees would roll.
   - ❑ c. visited a neighboring village.

8. In the 21st century there will probably be _____ in the types of transportation.
   - ❑ a. a reduction
   - ❑ b. an increase
   - ❑ c. no change

9. Advances in transportation have most likely had the greatest impact on the _____ of the population.
   - ❑ a. movement
   - ❑ b. size
   - ❑ c. patience

10. You can conclude from the article that the invention of the railroad
    - ❑ a. did little to impact the way people traveled.
    - ❑ b. helped open up trade between the eastern and western United States.
    - ❑ c. occurred after the invention of the internal combustion engine.

15   B   Incredible Inventors

Some things are so integral to our lives that we can't imagine how people ever lived without them. Some of the most significant inventions have involved automobile parts.

John Boyd Dunlop, a Scot, developed the pneumatic tire. This is a tire filled with air instead of a solid material. In 1888 he saw his son having trouble riding his tricycle over rough roads. Dunlop thought that he could help ease some of this discomfort by using a wheel filled with air. This tire was used on bicycles before it was used on cars and trucks. It is used by hundreds of millions of people today.

The phrase "the real McCoy" probably refers to an African-American inventor, Elijah McCoy. McCoy was the son of slaves. He was trained as a mechanical engineer. The only job he could find was putting wood into furnaces for the Michigan Central Railroad. Part of his job was to oil the moving parts when the trains stopped. The job was dangerous and time-consuming. He began work on a lubricating system that would allow engine parts to be oiled automatically while moving. His invention was patented in 1872. It worked so well that people began insisting that their machines have the "real McCoy" so that they would run more smoothly and safely.

Today's vehicles all benefit from the inventions of these two men.

1. Recognizing Words in Context

Find the word *integral* in the passage. One definition below is closest to the meaning of that word. One definition has the opposite or nearly opposite meaning. The remaining definition has a completely different meaning. Label the definitions C for *closest,* O for *opposite or nearly opposite,* and D for *different.*

_____ a. essential

_____ b. unimportant

_____ c. beautiful

2. Distinguishing Fact from Opinion

Two of the statements below present *facts,* which can be proved correct. The other statement is an *opinion,* which expresses someone's thoughts or beliefs. Label the statements F for *fact* and O for *opinion.*

_____ a. McCoy was an inventor.

_____ b. McCoy's lubricating system was patented in 1872.

_____ c. If Dunlop hadn't seen his son riding a tricycle, we would not have the pneumatic tire today.

3. Keeping Events in Order

Label the statements below 1, 2, and 3 to show the order in which the events happened.

_____ a. Dunlop decided to help his son.

_____ b. Dunlop created the pneumatic tire.

_____ c. Dunlop's son had a difficult time riding his tricycle.

4. Making Correct Inferences

Two of the statements below are correct *inferences,* or reasonable guesses. They are based on information in the passage. The other statement is an incorrect, or faulty, inference. Label the statements C for *correct* inference and F for *faulty* inference.

_____ a. McCoy was trained for a different job than the one he had with the railroad.

_____ b. Dunlop's son was the only child who had a hard time riding a tricycle.

_____ c. Inventors often get their ideas from problems in their daily lives.

5. Understanding Main Ideas

One of the statements below expresses the main idea of the passage. One statement is too general, or too broad. The other explains only part of the passage; it is too narrow. Label the statements M for *main idea,* B for *too broad,* and N for *too narrow.*

_____ a. Many inventions have contributed to the lives we lead today.

_____ b. McCoy and Dunlop made significant contributions to our current lives.

_____ c. McCoy was trained as a mechanical engineer.

Correct Answers, Part A _____

Correct Answers, Part B _____

Total Correct Answers _____

The Mighty Insect

Have you ever been at a picnic that was taken over by ants or at a ballgame where the mosquitoes seemed to outnumber the fans? If so, then you are already aware that insects are the dominant life form on Earth. A single city block or a single farm can contain millions of insects. What is even more remarkable is that each of these insects plays a valuable role in our planet's ecosystem. Insects are found in every region and environment—a few even live around oceans.

Insects are the main consumers of plant life on the planet. They also function as a vital part of the food chain. They are important for breaking down plant and animal material. They also serve as food for larger animal species.

We can learn about insects by studying how their bodies work. An insect's body has three parts: a head, a thorax, and an abdomen. The head, which includes antennae, is used primarily for eating and sense perception. It also serves as an information-processing center. The thorax provides the structural support for six legs and up to two pairs of wings. The abdomen is the place where digestion and reproduction occur.

Insects can adapt to many different environments. If insects are unable to live in their existing environment, they can change their needs to fit their surroundings. Insects require very little food and can live in small spaces. They are cold blooded, which means that their body temperature varies with the outside temperature. Insects have a hard outer shell called an exoskeleton. This shell helps them to adapt and also helps to protect them.

Humans have a complex relationship with insects. They provide us directly with products such as wax, silk, and honey. We benefit indirectly from their pollination of crops, flowers, and other plants. Pollination is necessary for plants to produce seeds.

However, some insects cause harm by destroying plants or spreading disease. We need to find ways to control the number of insects without interfering with the ways they are helpful. By learning about insects, we can find ways to manage them without affecting the delicate balance of our planet. We must always remember that all the creatures on Earth serve a purpose—even mosquitoes, which are an important food source for bats, birds, and other insects. So the next time an insect is bothering you, remember some of the valuable services insects perform.

Reading Time _____

Recalling Facts

1. The dominant life forms on Earth are
   - ❏ a. mammals.
   - ❏ b. insects.
   - ❏ c. trees.

2. One of the reasons an insect adapts easily to new surroundings is its
   - ❏ a. exoskeleton.
   - ❏ b. adapter.
   - ❏ c. abdomen.

3. The body temperature of insects changes according to their surroundings, because insects are
   - ❏ a. reptiles.
   - ❏ b. warm blooded.
   - ❏ c. cold blooded.

4. Insects provide us with such products as
   - ❏ a. silk.
   - ❏ b. rubber.
   - ❏ c. plastic.

5. The insect's abdomen is used for
   - ❏ a. information processing.
   - ❏ b. digestion and reproduction.
   - ❏ c. breathing and tasting.

Understanding Ideas

6. You can conclude from the article that, as a group, insects
   - ❏ a. will probably become extinct.
   - ❏ b. have been very successful at surviving.
   - ❏ c. are much more harmful than helpful.

7. You would be least likely to see insects in the
   - ❏ a. ocean.
   - ❏ b. air.
   - ❏ c. hills.

8. Pollination is helpful to humans because it
   - ❏ a. decreases the insect population.
   - ❏ b. makes flowers smell pleasant.
   - ❏ c. allows plants to produce seeds.

9. Because insects require very little food, it is easy for them to
   - ❏ a. avoid pesticides.
   - ❏ b. adapt to many environments.
   - ❏ c. hibernate in the winter.

10. You can conclude from the article that larger animals depend on insects
    - ❏ a. in many ways.
    - ❏ b. only occasionally.
    - ❏ c. for help with migration.

The dragonfly is one of the most ancient of all creatures on Earth. Fossils of dragonflies have been found that are as old as 250 million years. Why did the dragonfly survive while other species died out? Part of the reason is its efficient body design.

Dragonflies have long, slender abdomens and two pair of long, slender wings. The wings can work independently and alternately from each other. They allow the dragonfly to fly at speeds of up to 100 kilometers per hour (60 miles per hour). Dragonflies can hover, fly backward, stop instantly, and fly straight up in the air. They are truly aerial masters.

Dragonflies have two large compound eyes. *Compound* means "made up of many parts." One part looks up to the sky to see whether there is any danger while the other part scans the air below for prey. Each eye has nearly 30,000 lenses! Dragonflies can focus on objects 20 feet away. Dragonflies also have serrated teeth located in their mouth area. *Serrated* means "shaped like the teeth of a saw." Dragonflies eat many types of flying insects, including mosquitoes.

There are more than 400 species of dragonflies in North America. They are often beautifully colored in bright green, blue, red, or violet. Though its life span ranges from only two weeks to two months, the dragonfly plays an important role in the natural world by helping to control insect populations.

1. **Recognizing Words in Context**

   Find the word *aerial* in the passage. One definition below is closest to the meaning of that word. One definition has the opposite or nearly opposite meaning. The remaining definition has a completely different meaning. Label the definitions C for *closest,* O for *opposite or nearly opposite,* and D for *different.*

   _____ a. at high speed

   _____ b. on the ground

   _____ c. in the air

2. **Distinguishing Fact from Opinion**

   Two of the statements below present *facts,* which can be proved correct. The other statement is an *opinion,* which expresses someone's thoughts or beliefs. Label the statements F for *fact* and O for *opinion.*

   _____ a. Dragonflies have four wings.

   _____ b. Dragonflies have two compound eyes.

   _____ c. Dragonflies hover like graceful dancers.

3. Keeping Events in Order

Label the statements below 1, 2, and 3 to show the order in which the events happen.

_____ a. It spots a mosquito.

_____ b. The mosquito disappears into the dragonfly's long abdomen.

_____ c. The dragonfly uses its compound eyes to scan for prey.

4. Making Correct Inferences

Two of the statements below are correct *inferences,* or reasonable guesses. They are based on information in the passage. The other statement is an incorrect, or faulty, inference. Label the statements C for *correct* inference and F for *faulty* inference.

_____ a. Dragonflies evolved from ancient dragons.

_____ b. Dragonflies will most likely continue to adapt to survive long into the future.

_____ c. Dragonflies are skilled hunters of other flying insects.

5. Understanding Main Ideas

One of the statements below expresses the main idea of the passage. One statement is too general, or too broad. The other explains only part of the passage; it is too narrow. Label the statements M for *main idea,* B for *too broad,* and N for *too narrow.*

_____ a. Some flying insects are big eaters.

_____ b. Dragonflies have many characteristics that have helped them to survive over millions of years.

_____ c. Dragonflies have serrated teeth.

Correct Answers, Part A _____

Correct Answers, Part B _____

Total Correct Answers _____

Mountains

Throughout history, people have looked to the mountains for inspiration and recreation. Few things on Earth can match the beauty of mountains. Mountains come in many forms. In the southeastern United States, the mountains are covered in trees and grasses. In the southwestern United States, the mountains are large rock formations with very little greenery.

Earth is constantly changing, so mountain ranges are changing too. Just like people, mountains grow and change, only much more slowly! A mountain range can take millions of years to form. The mountains you see today will look very different millions of years from now.

Mountains are one of the major landforms on Earth. You can see them on every continent. There are even mountains on the ocean floor. Though each mountain is unique, geologists group mountains into four categories. These categories are volcanic, residual, fault-block, and folded.

Volcanic mountains are commonly known as volcanoes. They occur in areas where hot lava and magma have moved to the surface and pushed through Earth's crust. Forming volcanoes is the way Earth releases its heat and internal pressure. Mount Saint Helens is an example of a volcanic mountain.

Residual mountains occur when water and wind wear away weak parts of the land. Residual mountains often were created when a large body of water covered an area and then the water slowly receded. Parts of the Rocky Mountains are examples of residual mountains.

Fault-block mountains form along faults, which are deep breaks in Earth's crust. When forces within Earth push up material on one side of the fault, mountains are formed. The Sierra Nevada range is an example of fault-block mountains.

Folded mountains are the most common type. They are created by the collision of tectonic plates, the plates that make up Earth's crust. This collision pushes up enormous sections of land to form mountains. The Himalayas are folded mountains.

Mountains have diverse ecosystems. Many types of plants grow from the base to the peak. The foothills may have broad-leafed forests. As you climb higher, spruce trees may appear. The higher you climb, the colder it gets. Also, the higher you climb, the more the oxygen thins out. This causes the trees to thin out as well. Mountaintops support only sparse grasses and wildflowers. On the tallest mountains, the peaks are bare and covered with snow and ice.

Reading Time _____

Recalling Facts

1. Volcanic mountains are also known as
   - ❑ a. volcanoes.
   - ❑ b. crevices.
   - ❑ c. lava formations.

2. A mountain is a type of
   - ❑ a. fault.
   - ❑ b. landform.
   - ❑ c. continent.

3. Mount Saint Helens is an example of a
   - ❑ a. residual mountain.
   - ❑ b. fault-block mountain.
   - ❑ c. volcanic mountain.

4. The most common type of mountain is the
   - ❑ a. residual mountain.
   - ❑ b. folded mountain.
   - ❑ c. fault-block mountain.

5. The ecosystem of a mountain is very
   - ❑ a. diverse.
   - ❑ b. sparse.
   - ❑ c. fertile.

Understanding Ideas

6. From the information in the article, you can conclude that
   - ❑ a. all mountains look the same.
   - ❑ b. mountains have different appearances based on their location.
   - ❑ c. the highest mountains are on the ocean floor.

7. If a folded mountain forms, you can assume that
   - ❑ a. large sections of Earth's crust have collided.
   - ❑ b. a major volcanic eruption has occurred.
   - ❑ c. a large lake has eroded minerals from a rock formation.

8. If you are at the top of a high mountain and there is very little grass, you can assume
   - ❑ a. there is very little oxygen.
   - ❑ b. there is too much carbon dioxide.
   - ❑ c. you are on a residual mountain.

9. As you climb a mountain, you will most likely notice
   - ❑ a. an increase in the number of plants.
   - ❑ b. no change in the plants.
   - ❑ c. a wide variety of plants.

10. You could assume that over the next million years
    - ❑ a. mountains will continue to change.
    - ❑ b. mountains will remain the same.
    - ❑ c. no more mountains will be created.

Volunteers play a major role in helping to keep hiking trails safe for visitors. Volunteer groups work under the supervision of the U.S. Forest Service. They perform a number of jobs to help forest rangers maintain the trails.

The volunteers walk the trails to make sure nothing is blocking the paths. They may even go out in the winter to monitor the trails. When they find debris or garbage, they remove it from the area. They may also help to repair bridges or move fallen trees. After a storm, there is always lots of work to do, especially with fallen branches. Volunteers also observe wildlife and may be the first ones to notice changes in the environment. The things the volunteers observe help the forest service create programs that make the best use of its time and resources.

If you're not a big hiking fan, you can still help out. Many volunteer activities are indoors. You might help answer phones. Or you could help educate the community about conservation efforts. If you enjoy the outdoors, helping at your local park may be the perfect thing for you. Call your local parks and recreation department. They can help you find volunteer jobs in your area.

1. **Recognizing Words in Context**

   Find the word *maintain* in the passage. One definition below is closest to the meaning of that word. One definition has the opposite or nearly opposite meaning. The remaining definition has a completely different meaning. Label the definitions C for *closest,* O for *opposite or nearly opposite,* and D for *different.*

   _____ a. compose

   _____ b. destroy

   _____ c. preserve

2. **Distinguishing Fact from Opinion**

   Two of the statements below present *facts,* which can be proved correct. The other statement is an *opinion,* which expresses someone's thoughts or beliefs. Label the statements F for *fact* and O for *opinion.*

   _____ a. Volunteers help to keep the trails safe.

   _____ b. Volunteers are a key part of the U.S. Forest Service.

   _____ c. Volunteers may help answer phones.

3. Keeping Events in Order

Label the statements below 1, 2, and 3 to show the order in which the events happen.

_____ a. A storm causes trails to become cluttered.

_____ b. Volunteers clear away the debris on the paths.

_____ c. A team of volunteers is identified and assembled.

4. Making Correct Inferences

Two of the statements below are correct *inferences,* or reasonable guesses. They are based on information in the passage. The other statement is an incorrect, or faulty, inference. Label the statements C for *correct* inference and F for *faulty* inference.

_____ a. Without the help of volunteers, park trails would not be as well maintained.

_____ b. Volunteers can help people learn how to care for the trails.

_____ c. If no one volunteers to help with the trails, the parks will close.

5. Understanding Main Ideas

One of the statements below expresses the main idea of the passage. One statement is too general, or too broad. The other explains only part of the passage; it is too narrow. Label the statements M for *main idea,* B for *too broad,* and N for *too narrow.*

_____ a. Volunteers help clear away debris.

_____ b. Volunteers play a major role in helping to keep trails safe for visitors.

_____ c. Hiking trails are important for recreation.

Correct Answers, Part A _____

Correct Answers, Part B _____

Total Correct Answers _____

How can a tree go from being the height of a person to the height of a five-story building? Like all living things, trees are made up of cells. Many types of cells work together to make up a tall tree.

Just like most other plants, trees have three main parts: the roots, the stem, and the leaves. The roots run deep in the ground to help support the tree. They absorb water and minerals such as nitrogen and calcium from the soil to help the tree grow.

The stem helps lift the leaves and flowers to the light. It's important that the leaves reach the sunlight, because the leaves need light to do their job of producing food for the tree. The stem also transports water and food to and from different parts of the tree. The stem of a tree consists of its trunk and branches.

The leaves absorb carbon dioxide and solar energy from the atmosphere and combine them with water and minerals to form carbohydrates. These carbohydrates, which include starch and sugar, provide food for other parts of the plant. Oxygen left over from this process is released into the atmosphere. This process is called photosynthesis. Almost every living thing depends on photosynthesis for oxygen so it can breathe.

When a tree grows in the spring, a layer of cells called the cambium begins dividing very quickly. These new cells form on both the inside and the outside of the cambium layer. They add to the overall diameter of the tree. The cells that move to the outside of the cambium layer become part of the phloem. Phloem cells carry food produced in the leaves to the branches, trunk, and roots. Each year some phloem dies and becomes part of the bark.

Most of the new cells form on the inside of the cambium layer. These cells become xylem cells and make up most of the growth of the diameter of the tree. It's the job of the xylem cells to carry water and nutrients from the roots to the leaves.

Trees continue to grow until old age. Their diameters always increase, but the vertical growth tapers off because the trees have difficulty transporting nutrients to branches that are far from the roots. The top branches eventually dry out.

Trees provide more than just shade—they help provide us with the breath of life!

Reading Time _____

Recalling Facts

1. Trees are made up of
   - ❏ a. sticks.
   - ❏ b. bones.
   - ❏ c. cells.

2. The _____ carries water and minerals from the roots to the leaves.
   - ❏ a. cambium layer
   - ❏ b. xylem cells
   - ❏ c. phloem cells

3. The most important element needed for leaves to produce food for the tree is
   - ❏ a. a low temperature.
   - ❏ b. sunlight.
   - ❏ c. space.

4. A tree feeds on
   - ❏ a. oxygen.
   - ❏ b. nitrogen.
   - ❏ c. carbohydrates.

5. By what process do the leaves create food?
   - ❏ a. photosynthesis
   - ❏ b. mineral absorption
   - ❏ c. xylem process

Understanding Ideas

6. When new cells form on both sides of the cambium layer, the diameter of the tree
   - ❏ a. decreases.
   - ❏ b. increases.
   - ❏ c. remains the same.

7. The article suggests that a tree with dry top branches is
   - ❏ a. old.
   - ❏ b. young.
   - ❏ c. dead.

8. If tree A has a diameter of 1 meter and tree B has a diameter of 2 meters, it's most likely that
   - ❏ a. tree B is older than tree A.
   - ❏ b. tree B is younger than tree A.
   - ❏ c. both trees are the same age

9. From the article, you can assume that if there were no trees there would be
   - ❏ a. more oxygen.
   - ❏ b. no change in the amount of oxygen.
   - ❏ c. less oxygen.

10. You can conclude from the article that photosynthesis is important
    - ❏ a. only to humans.
    - ❏ b. only to trees.
    - ❏ c. to trees and humans.

18   B   Tree Rings: Diary of a Life

Trees hold many secrets in their trunks. Tree rings can help us not only determine how old the tree is but also tell the natural history of an area. The science of studying tree rings is called dendrochronology. A tree ring is simply a layer of wood produced during one growing season. The layer is produced in springtime. During a good year with plenty of food and rainfall, a tree will add a thick layer of tissue that shows up as a fat tree ring. In years where the resources are scarce, the tree will produce only a thin ring.

Trees also respond to weather patterns. Temperature, rainfall, and other environmental conditions—such as fires—can affect the tree's growth and alter the size of the tree ring. The tree rings can also reflect a year in which there were insect plagues. Though all trees don't respond to environmental changes in the same way, trees can be a valuable source for learning about our past. Scientists can try to determine what natural conditions occurred during times of heavy fires or droughts.

The bristlecone pines in the Rocky Mountains are among the oldest living things on Earth. Some are more than 5,000 years old. Scientists studying global weather patterns hope to use these trees to predict future weather patterns and climate changes. The key to our future may well have been written in the past.

1. **Recognizing Words in Context**
    Find the word *affect* in the passage. One definition below is closest to the meaning of that word. One definition has the opposite or nearly opposite meaning. The remaining definition has a completely different meaning. Label the definitions C for *closest,* O for *opposite or nearly opposite,* and D for *different.*

    _____ a. influence

    _____ b. keep the same

    _____ c. invent

2. **Distinguishing Fact from Opinion**
    Two of the statements below present *facts,* which can be proved correct. The other statement is an *opinion,* which expresses someone's thoughts or beliefs. Label the statements F for *fact* and O for *opinion.*

    _____ a. If resources are scarce, trees will produce only a thin ring.

    _____ b. Tree rings can show us when natural disasters occurred.

    _____ c. Trees are the best method of understanding past weather patterns.

3. Keeping Events in Order

Label the statements below 1, 2, and 3 to show the order in which the events happen.

_____ a. Dendrochronologists study the rings and draw conclusions.

_____ b. Trees produce thin tree rings.

_____ c. A drought year occurs.

4. Making Correct Inferences

Two of the statements below are correct *inferences,* or reasonable guesses. They are based on information in the passage. The other statement is an incorrect, or faulty, inference. Label the statements C for *correct* inference and F for *faulty* inference.

_____ a. Dendrochronologists are interested in natural history.

_____ b. Tree rings provide information about insect damage.

_____ c. Tree rings provide a record of when tornadoes hit an area.

5. Understanding Main Ideas

One of the statements below expresses the main idea of the passage. One statement is too general, or too broad. The other explains only part of the passage; it is too narrow. Label the statements M for *main idea,* B for *too broad,* and N for *too narrow.*

_____ a. Tree rings can provide us with important information about our past and future.

_____ b. A tree ring forms in springtime.

_____ c. Many things occur during the life of a tree.

Correct Answers, Part A _____

Correct Answers, Part B _____

Total Correct Answers _____

Spectacular displays of lightning have awed people for centuries. Although lightning can be deadly at times, it also can be helpful.

Lightning is a charge of electricity that comes from clouds. At any given moment, there is probably lightning flashing someplace in the world. There are thousands of lightning strikes each day.

Lightning occurs because thunderstorm clouds contain strong upward winds called updrafts. The updrafts push rain droplets up into the cold upper part of a cloud, where the droplets freeze into ice particles and begin to fall back down. The interaction between ice particles and water droplets separates the electric charge within molecules into positive and negative parts. The top of the cloud becomes positively charged, and the middle of the cloud becomes negatively charged. When the buildup of energy is great enough, the oppositely charged particles attract each other. They discharge their energy as a bolt of lightning.

Cloud-to-ground lightning is the most dangerous type of lightning. When the electrical charge in the middle of the cloud is strong enough, the cloud releases channels of charged air called leaders. Leaders reach down in search of positively charged air. They attract other charged channels, called streamers, from the ground. When the leaders and streamers meet, the result is lightning.

Most lightning does not strike the ground. Lightning discharges can occur within the same cloud. This is called intracloud lightning. Lightning also strikes from cloud to cloud. This is called intercloud lightning. "Dry" lightning occurs when lightning strikes from a cloud that is not making rain. This type of lightning can cause forest fires because there is no rain.

Forest fires are not necessarily bad, however. They help the ecosystem by burning off deadwood and plant life. This helps clear away debris for new growth. Forest fires have occurred naturally for millions of years. When people began trying to prevent forest fires, they thought lightning strikes were a problem. Now people are recognizing the importance of these naturally occurring fires for our planet's health. Lightning also puts nitrogen in the ground. Nitrogen is necessary to help plants grow.

If you count the seconds between the flash of lightning and the rumble of thunder, you can see how far away lightning struck. Five seconds equals 1.6 kilometers (1 mile). The next time you see lightning, start counting! When thunder rumbles, you will know how far away lightning struck.

Reading Time _____

Recalling Facts

1. Lightning strikes someplace on Earth
   - ❏ a. thousands of times each day.
   - ❏ b. once every 10 minutes.
   - ❏ c. 10,000 times per second.

2. The most dangerous type of lightning is
   - ❏ a. intercloud lightning.
   - ❏ b. intracloud lightning.
   - ❏ c. cloud-to-ground lightning.

3. Lightning from clouds that don't make rain is called
   - ❏ a. wet lightning.
   - ❏ b. dry lightning.
   - ❏ c. cloud lightning.

4. Within a cloud, oppositely charged particles
   - ❏ a. attract each other.
   - ❏ b. repel each other.
   - ❏ c. remain neutral.

5. Lightning discharges within the same cloud are called
   - ❏ a. cloud-to-ground lightning.
   - ❏ b. intracloud lightning.
   - ❏ c. intercloud lightning.

Understanding Ideas

6. You can conclude from the article that a key component to a lightning strike is
   - ❏ a. wind.
   - ❏ b. clouds.
   - ❏ c. rain.

7. You can assume from the article that
   - ❏ a. all lightning strikes the ground.
   - ❏ b. rain always accompanies lightning strikes.
   - ❏ c. lightning strikes create healthier forests.

8. If you witness a bolt of lightning rather than a flash, you are most likely seeing
   - ❏ a. dry lightning.
   - ❏ b. intracloud lightning.
   - ❏ c. cloud-to-ground lightning.

9. If you count 25 seconds between the flash of lightning and the thunder rumble, then you can assume the lightning strike is about
   - ❏ a. 1.6 kilometers away.
   - ❏ b. 8 kilometers away.
   - ❏ c. 80 kilometers away.

10. Which of the following is probably not true about forest fires?
    - ❏ a. A forest fire caused by an unattended campfire is a naturally occurring fire.
    - ❏ b. Forest fires can be beneficial to the forest.
    - ❏ c. Beliefs about naturally occurring forest fires have changed.

Lightning Safety

Lightning strikes in many parts of the world. Lightning is an electric charge in a thunderstorm that is powerful enough to hurt or kill people. Here are a few basic safety rules to follow if you find yourself in a thunderstorm.

First, find shelter. Get inside a building or a car. Don't stand under a tree. If you're in a car, stay away from metal surfaces that can conduct electricity. Lightning can strike as far away as 16 kilometers (10 miles) from the center of the storm. Just because lightning and thunder seem far away, you should not assume that there is no danger. Remember that lightning will generally strike the highest place in an area. Don't climb trees or play outside during a thunderstorm.

Golfers are often struck by lightning when they continue to play golf during a thunderstorm. They might think that they aren't in danger if it isn't raining. This is not true. The golf clubs can function as lightning rods.

If you're inside, don't talk on the phone. Lightning can travel through the telephone wires and strike you while you're talking. Turn off TVs, computers, and other appliances and stay away from them. Water is also a conductor of electricity. Don't take a shower and stay away from sinks. Practice these basic safety rules and use your common sense to stay safe.

1. Recognizing Words in Context

Find the word *conduct* in the passage. One definition below is closest to the meaning of that word. One definition has the opposite or nearly opposite meaning. The remaining definition has a completely different meaning. Label the definitions C for *closest,* O for *opposite or nearly opposite,* and D for *different.*

_____ a. carry

_____ b. resist

_____ c. charge

2. Distinguishing Fact from Opinion

Two of the statements below present *facts,* which can be proved correct. The other statement is an *opinion,* which expresses someone's thoughts or beliefs. Label the statements F for *fact* and O for *opinion.*

_____ a. Lightning can strike up to 16 kilometers from a storm.

_____ b. Golfers are not cautious enough about thunder-storms.

_____ c. Lightning usually strikes the highest point in an area.

3. Keeping Events in Order

Label the statements below 1, 2, and 3 to show the order in which the events happen.

_____ a. Lightning travels through phone lines.

_____ b. Lightning strikes someone talking on the phone.

_____ c. A thunderstorm approaches an area.

4. Making Correct Inferences

Two of the statements below are correct *inferences*, or reasonable guesses. They are based on information in the passage. The other statement is an incorrect, or faulty, inference. Label the statements C for *correct* inference and F for *faulty* inference.

_____ a. It is safer to be in a car than to stand under a tree during a lightning storm.

_____ b. A golf club can conduct lightning.

_____ c. If it isn't raining, you're safe from lightning strikes.

5. Understanding Main Ideas

One of the statements below expresses the main idea of the passage. One statement is too general, or too broad. The other explains only part of the passage; it is too narrow. Label the statements M for *main idea*, B for *too broad*, and N for *too narrow*.

_____ a. Following basic safety rules can help keep you safe from lightning.

_____ b. Lightning is one type of weather event that can kill people.

_____ c. Lightning can travel through water.

Correct Answers, Part A _____

Correct Answers, Part B _____

Total Correct Answers _____

Space Mysteries

Black holes and quasars are two of the mysteries of our universe. A black hole, once called a frozen star, is believed to arise from the death of a star. It is a region of space that has so much mass concentrated in it that nearby objects have no way to escape its gravitational pull.

A black hole has a strange property called an event horizon. This is a spherical surface that marks the edge of the black hole. Objects can move toward the event horizon, but they cannot move away from it once they have crossed it. The event horizon is the place where the escape velocity equals the speed of light. Outside the horizon, the escape velocity is less than the speed of light. This means an object that is outside the horizon can escape the pull of the black hole. But if the object is inside the horizon, it can't escape the pull of gravity because nothing can move faster than the speed of light.

Escape velocity is also related to the gravitational pull of a planet. On Earth, if you throw an object into the air, it will travel upward but then get pulled back down by gravity. But if the object is traveling fast enough—as fast as a rocket, for example—it can escape from Earth's atmosphere and fly into space.

The more mass a planet has, the larger its escape velocity. Earth's escape velocity is about 40,000 kilometers per hour (25,000 miles per hour). A black hole has a much higher escape velocity.

Another oddity of the universe is the quasar. *Quasar* stands for "quasi-stellar radio sources." Quasars were discovered when scientists aimed radio telescopes toward the sky. They found that radio waves were coming from sources in outer space. Some of these sources, or quasars, could be identified as distant galaxies or the remnants of exploded stars called supernovas. Others could not be identified. Scientists think quasars may be the bright centers of very distant galaxies. They think quasars are related to black holes, because matter falling into a black hole could result in a very hot region where huge energies are released. This energy would produce the emitted light seen as quasars.

Astronomy is constantly changing as we get more information about the universe. One day we may know exactly what a quasar is. One day we may travel close to a black hole, but not too close!

Reading Time _____

Recalling Facts

1. Scientists believe black holes are formed by
   - ❏ a. the death of a star.
   - ❏ b. planets colliding.
   - ❏ c. lost satellites.

2. Black holes were once called
   - ❏ a. frozen stars.
   - ❏ b. black death.
   - ❏ c. time warp.

3. The spherical surface that marks the boundary of a black hole is the
   - ❏ a. quasar.
   - ❏ b. escape velocity.
   - ❏ c. event horizon.

4. Earth's escape velocity is
   - ❏ a. 40,000 mph.
   - ❏ b. 40,000 kph.
   - ❏ c. 24,000 kph.

5. Quasars emit
   - ❏ a. event horizons.
   - ❏ b. black holes.
   - ❏ c. radio waves.

Understanding Ideas

6. From this reading, you can conclude that the information we know about space
   - ❏ a. never changes.
   - ❏ b. always changes.
   - ❏ c. remains constant for long periods of time.

7. You can infer that a radio telescope is something that can
   - ❏ a. receive radio waves.
   - ❏ b. be more powerful than the Hubble telescope.
   - ❏ c. give us a very accurate picture of event horizons.

8. Escape velocity could be described as the
   - ❏ a. speed needed to escape the pull of gravity.
   - ❏ b. gravity needed to enter a black hole.
   - ❏ c. force needed to create a black hole.

9. From the passage, you can conclude that an important quality for an astronomer is
   - ❏ a. flexibility.
   - ❏ b. intolerance.
   - ❏ c. wealth.

10. You can assume that in the future
    - ❏ a. we will know less about space than we do today.
    - ❏ b. we will prove all of our current theories about space correct.
    - ❏ c. we may find some of the things we believe today about space are false.

Mars, Anyone?

Mars is among the planets that are closest to Earth. For most of human history, Mars has been a place that has inspired unusual stories and much curiosity. Scientists are eager to find out whether there is evidence of life on Mars. If people travel to Mars some day, it will be a tremendous engineering feat and a source of pride for human beings.

The astronauts on a journey to Mars would have to spend more than a year away from home. They would be confined in very close quarters in the the spacecraft for nine months each way. Think of how hard it is to travel in the backseat of the car with your little brother or sister! Although the spacecraft would be larger than a minivan, it wouldn't be much bigger than a 747 aircraft.

Once the astronauts passed the Moon, they would be farther into space than any human being has ever been before. Depending on the orbit of the spacecraft, Earth could be as far as 400 million kilometers (250 million miles) away. The astronauts could not even see the blue and green of Earth. They would look out the spacecraft's window and see only darkness. Communication with Earth would be limited.

Psychologists are studying personality types to determine what kind of person might be best suited for a mission to Mars. A great deal of research is needed to create a successful human space mission to Mars.

1. **Recognizing Words in Context**
   Find the word *confined* in the passage. One definition below is closest to the meaning of that word. One definition has the opposite or nearly opposite meaning. The remaining definition has a completely different meaning. Label the definitions C for *closest,* O for *opposite or nearly opposite,* and D for *different.*

   _____ a. freed

   _____ b. rewarded

   _____ c. limited

2. **Distinguishing Fact from Opinion**
   Two of the statements below present *facts,* which can be proved correct. The other statement is an *opinion,* which expresses someone's thoughts or beliefs. Label the statements F for *fact* and O for *opinion.*

   _____ a. The Moon is closer to Earth than Mars is.

   _____ b. If astronauts can make it to Mars and back, they will be heroes.

   _____ c. No astronaut has traveled beyond the Moon.

3. Keeping Events in Order

Label the statements below 1, 2, and 3 to show the order in which the events happen.

_____ a. Astronauts are near the Moon.

_____ b. Astronauts board a spacecraft on Earth.

_____ c. Astronauts orbit Mars.

4. Making Correct Inferences

Two of the statements below are correct *inferences,* or reasonable guesses. They are based on information in the passage. The other statement is an incorrect, or faulty, inference. Label the statements C for *correct* inference and F for *faulty* inference.

_____ a. Anyone with the right training would make a good candidate for a journey to Mars.

_____ b. Not all personality types would be well suited for a trip to Mars.

_____ c. A trip on the space shuttle would be good training for a mission to Mars.

5. Understanding Main Ideas

One of the statements below expresses the main idea of the passage. One statement is too general, or too broad. The other explains only part of the passage; it is too narrow. Label the statements M for *main idea,* B for *too broad,* and N for *too narrow.*

_____ a. Astronauts will not be able to see Earth from the spacecraft.

_____ b. Someday human beings may travel to another planet.

_____ c. A trip to Mars will require engineering and psychological preparation.

Correct Answers, Part A _____

Correct Answers, Part B _____

Total Correct Answers _____

The History of Vaccinations

The word *vaccination* comes from the Latin word *vacca*, meaning "cow." An Englishman named Edward Jenner coined this term. He noticed that dairy workers who were exposed to a disease called cowpox did not get smallpox, a much more serious disease that killed many people. Jenner thought that if he intentionally infected people with cowpox virus, it would protect them from smallpox. He began work to prove his theory. He gave the first smallpox vaccination in 1796.

Vaccinations, also called immunizations, give some control over the spread of disease. A vaccination puts a weakened form of a pathogen into a person's body. Pathogens, which include viruses, are tiny groups of cells that cause diseases. The body learns to recognize the pathogen. It creates a type of protein, called an antibody, that fights the pathogen. Then, if the person is exposed to a stronger form of the pathogen, his or her immune system will already know how to fight it.

In the 19th century, Louis Pasteur of France introduced the "germ theory" of disease. He felt that disease could pass from person to person by small microorganisms called germs. Prior to the development of this theory, hospitals were not very clean. Pasteur also developed the vaccine for rabies.

One of the most important medical breakthroughs of the 20th century belonged to Jonas Salk. He grew polio viruses in living tissues in a laboratory. This produced a polio vaccine. It was licensed in 1955. Prior to this development, polio had killed or crippled millions of children worldwide.

Some diseases, like malaria and influenza, have been quite challenging to medical researchers. The pathogens that cause them are able to mutate, or change. This means that when scientists learn how to fight one strain, or type, of the pathogen, there are already many other strains to fight.

We use immunization today for several reasons. We can protect large groups of people against serious diseases that are common where they live. We can also protect travelers against diseases that are common in the areas to which they are going. In addition, we can immunize to protect groups, such as senior citizens and children, who are particularly vulnerable to certain diseases.

In the United States, schools require proof of vaccination before students can enroll. These requirements may include vaccination against such diseases as polio, diphtheria, measles, mumps, rubella, and tetanus. Combating disease remains one of the greatest challenges for humankind.

Reading Time _____

Recalling Facts

1. The first smallpox vaccination was administered in
   - ❏ a. 1776.
   - ❏ b. 1796.
   - ❏ c. 1867.

2. *Vaccination* comes from the Latin word for
   - ❏ a. cow.
   - ❏ b. disease.
   - ❏ c. cure.

3. Louis Pasteur developed the vaccine for
   - ❏ a. rabies.
   - ❏ b. tetanus.
   - ❏ c. measles.

4. Groups that are especially vulnerable to disease include children and
   - ❏ a. physicians.
   - ❏ b. young adults.
   - ❏ c. senior citizens.

5. The polio vaccine was developed by
   - ❏ a. Jonas Salk.
   - ❏ b. Louis Pasteur.
   - ❏ c. Edward Jenner.

Understanding Ideas

6. You can assume that
   - ❏ a. we have nothing else to learn about diseases.
   - ❏ b. all diseases behave the same way.
   - ❏ c. the more we learn about diseases, the more effectively we will be able to combat them.

7. You can conclude from the article that as we learn more about diseases
   - ❏ a. there will be no change in the quality of immunizations.
   - ❏ b. immunizations will be less effective
   - ❏ c. immunizations will be more effective.

8. Understanding how germs are spread led to
   - ❏ a. cleaner hospitals.
   - ❏ b. a rise in smallpox infections.
   - ❏ c. more people becoming doctors.

9. Which of the following virus traits would be most likely to present a challenge to scientists searching for a vaccine?
   - ❏ a. They can be airborne.
   - ❏ b. They can mutate.
   - ❏ c. They can be contagious.

10. If you were planning a trip to a foreign country, what might you do to help yourself stay healthy during the trip?
    - ❏ a. Research recommended vaccinations.
    - ❏ b. Call your travel agent about places to visit.
    - ❏ c. Investigate the kinds of restaurants in that region.

What You Should Know About Rabies

Rabies is a viral disease that affects the central nervous system. Only a few cases in the United States appear each year in humans. However, the disease is almost always fatal if a person does not receive vaccine within two days of exposure. These are some basic safety guidelines you should know to help keep yourself safe from rabies.

Always stay away from unknown animals. Watch for animals that are behaving oddly. If a skunk or a raccoon is walking down the sidewalk in broad daylight, this is abnormal behavior. Avoid this animal and tell an adult about it. Rabies is most often spread by a bite, but it can also be spread through scratches and contact with animal saliva. Rabies is not found only in dogs. It is found in a variety of animals, including raccoons, foxes, skunks, and cats, among others. It is found most often in bats

Some of the signs of rabies in animals are chewing at the bite site, fever, and slow eye reflexes. As the disease progresses, the animal experiences aggression and seizures. After this, paralysis develops in the infected limb. This is followed by drooling, foaming at the mouth, coma, and death.

If you have physical contact with an animal displaying any of these symptoms, get to a doctor immediately for treatment. Practice common sense. Stay away from stray animals. Vaccinate your pets. Although it is rare for humans to contract the disease, it is important to practice basic safety precautions.

1. Recognizing Words in Context

Find the word *abnormal* in the passage. One definition below is closest to the meaning of that word. One definition has the opposite or nearly opposite meaning. The remaining definition has a completely different meaning. Label the definitions C for *closest*, O for *opposite or nearly opposite*, and D for *different*.

_____ a. pretty

_____ b. unusual

_____ c. common

2. Distinguishing Fact from Opinion

Two of the statements below present *facts*, which can be proved correct. The other statement is an *opinion*, which expresses someone's thoughts or beliefs. Label the statements F for *fact* and O for *opinion*.

_____ a. Rabies is most often spread by a bite.

_____ b. There are few cases of rabies in humans each year.

_____ c. Rabies is not as dangerous as hepatitis.

3. Keeping Events in Order

Label the statements below 1, 2, and 3 to show the order in which the events happen.

_____ a. The bat is tested for rabies.

_____ b. A bat is flying around a house in the middle of the day.

_____ c. The local animal patrol office is alerted.

4. Making Correct Inferences

Two of the statements below are correct *inferences,* or reasonable guesses. They are based on information in the passage. The other statement is an incorrect, or faulty, inference. Label the statements C for *correct* inference and F for *faulty* inference.

_____ a. Rabid animals often display unusual behavior.

_____ b. Bats are more dangerous than dogs are.

_____ c. If a rabid animal bites you and you do not get medical treatment, you have little chance of surviving.

5. Understanding Main Ideas

One of the statements below expresses the main idea of the passage. One statement is too general, or too broad. The other explains only part of the passage; it is too narrow. Label the statements M for *main idea,* B for *too broad,* and N for *too narrow.*

_____ a. Rabies is a dangerous disease.

_____ b. A rabid dog will chew at the site of a bite.

_____ c. Following basic precautions can help keep you safe from rabies.

Correct Answers, Part A _____

Correct Answers, Part B _____

Total Correct Answers _____

Energy from the Sun

One of the best ways we have of making sure there is enough energy for the growing needs of the world is to find alternative sources of energy. The Sun is a natural place to look. People have been using the Sun as a source of energy for thousands of years.

The Sun is a renewable energy resource. We are trying to find ways to use the Sun's energy to replace some of the nonrenewable energy we get from fossil fuels, such as petroleum. Fossil fuels, our main source of energy, can be used only once.

The Sun's energy can be used in several ways. One way is in solar water heaters. In a solar water heater, water pipes are attached to a black solar panel that is attached to the back of a clear plastic box. When sunlight shines through the plastic, it warms the panel and the water inside the pipes.

Power plants that use solar energy have curved mirrors that focus sunlight on a water pipe. Soon the water in the pipe gets so hot it becomes steam. The steam is used to turn a turbine to make electricity. Since solar energy can only be made when the Sun is shining, some solar energy plants use natural gas to boil the water at night. Then the plant is able to produce electricity 24 hours a day.

Sunlight can also be changed directly into electricity using photovoltaic cells. These cells change sunlight into electricity for lights and appliances. They can also store solar energy in batteries that may be used to light a roadside billboard or a streetlight.

Solar energy is already widely used in California and Arizona. Those states have many days of sunlight each year. Places that have a good deal of sunshine year-round are the best places to start changing to solar energy. Many cities provide financial incentives for people to make their homes more energy efficient. If you drive by a house and see large dark glass panels on the south side of the roof, you're seeing a home that is using solar energy.

Today, converting to solar energy can be too costly for many families. Also, in areas where there is not a great deal of sunlight, there may not be enough power available to meet the need. But as our need for energy grows, more people will take advantage of this natural power source.

Reading Time _____

Recalling Facts

1. When sunlight strikes solar panels, it generates
   - ❑ a. atoms.
   - ❑ b. friction.
   - ❑ c. heat.

2. Energy from the Sun is a
   - ❑ a. renewable resource.
   - ❑ b. nonrenewable resource
   - ❑ c. type of fossil fuel.

3. A streetlight can be lit using energy from
   - ❑ a. digital images.
   - ❑ b. flashlights.
   - ❑ c. photovoltaic cells.

4. We currently get most of our energy from
   - ❑ a. solar power plants.
   - ❑ b. fossil fuels.
   - ❑ c. hydroelectric power plants.

5. To operate 24 hours a day, some solar power plants generate energy using
   - ❑ a. kerosene.
   - ❑ b. wood.
   - ❑ c. natural gas.

Understanding Ideas

6. If solar energy were less expensive, what would most likely happen to its usage?
   - ❑ a. Usage would increase.
   - ❑ b. Usage would decrease.
   - ❑ c. Usage would remain the same.

7. On which of the following days would solar energy most likely be least effective?
   - ❑ a. a hot day with clear skies
   - ❑ b. a warm, cloudy day
   - ❑ c. a cold day with clear skies

8. You can conclude from the article that solar energy
   - ❑ a. will be too costly to use.
   - ❑ b. will be our only alternative for future energy needs.
   - ❑ c. is an important renewable energy source.

9. Besides using solar energy, what is another way to use less fossil-fuel energy?
   - ❑ a. Use petroleum instead of coal.
   - ❑ b. Conserve energy.
   - ❑ c. Use premium gasoline instead of regular unleaded gasoline.

10. It is safe to assume that as our need for energy increases
    - ❑ a. we will find new and better ways of using solar energy.
    - ❑ b. there will be a reduced need for alternative fuel sources.
    - ❑ c. fossil fuels will become more plentiful.

What if it were suddenly dark outside in the middle of the day? What if birds stopped singing? What if crickets began their night songs? If all of these things were happening, you would be experiencing a total solar eclipse.

What causes a total solar eclipse? It happens when the Moon passes directly between the orbits of Earth and the Sun. Daylight changes eerily to darkness. Animals stop what they're doing and prepare for sleep. Some animals become confused or agitated. Nocturnal animals wake up.

Solar eclipses begin gradually. You may not even notice what is happening. There's just a slight change of light. You might think there's an approaching storm. But as the eclipse progresses, it moves very quickly to total darkness.

When the Moon moves directly in front of the Sun, totally obscuring it, the Sun's corona comes into view. This corona looks like a pearly white halo. It is only visible during a total eclipse. Seeing the corona is the high point of the eclipse for most people.

Total solar eclipses occur about 70 times each century. Not everyone on the planet can see a particular eclipse, however. You have to be at a specific location on the planet to view it. This location is called the path of totality. Because eclipses are so rare, you should take the time to see an eclipse if an opportunity occurs. But never look directly at an eclipse—you might damage your eyes.

1. **Recognizing Words in Context**
   Find the word *obscuring* in the passage. One definition below is closest to the meaning of that word. One definition has the opposite or nearly opposite meaning. The remaining definition has a completely different meaning. Label the definitions C for *closest*, O for *opposite or nearly opposite*, and D for *different*.

   _____ a. blocking

   _____ b. revealing

   _____ c. announcing

2. **Distinguishing Fact from Opinion**
   Two of the statements below present *facts*, which can be proved correct. The other statement is an *opinion*, which expresses someone's thoughts or beliefs. Label the statements F for *fact* and O for *opinion*.

   _____ a. A total solar eclipse is an amazing sight.

   _____ b. When a solar eclipse occurs, many animals think night has arrived.

   _____ c. Solar eclipses happen about 70 times a century.

3. **Keeping Events in Order**

   Label the statements below 1, 2, and 3 to show the order in which the events happen.

   _____ a. The Moon begins to block out the Sun.

   _____ b. The Sun's corona is visible.

   _____ c. It gets bright outside again.

4. **Making Correct Inferences**

   Two of the statements below are correct *inferences,* or reasonable guesses. They are based on information in the passage. The other statement is an incorrect, or faulty, inference. Label the statements C for *correct* inference and F for *faulty* inference.

   _____ a. When an eclipse occurs, not all people can see it.

   _____ b. When a total solar eclipse occurs, daylight turns to darkness.

   _____ c. The temperature drops at least 40 degrees during an eclipse.

5. **Understanding Main Ideas**

   One of the statements below expresses the main idea of the passage. One statement is too general, or too broad. The other explains only part of the passage; it is too narrow. Label the statements M for *main idea,* B for *too broad,* and N for *too narrow.*

   _____ a. Many fascinating events happen in the solar system.

   _____ b. Watching the corona come into view is the highlight of an eclipse.

   _____ c. A solar eclipse has many unique characteristics.

Correct Answers, Part A _____

Correct Answers, Part B _____

Total Correct Answers _____

Fire and the Forest Ecosystem

You've likely been told by your parents not to play with fire. Fire can be dangerous. However, fire is also a natural part of the world we live in. Some fires are very healthy and helpful to our planet.

Until the 20th century, people in the United States were not very concerned about forest fires. Almost all such fires were naturally occurring. This means they were started by natural means, such as lightning strikes. Naturally occurring fires are a part of our ecosystem.

Around 1900, people began to think that forest fires needed to be prevented. The process of preventing forest fires is called fire suppression. When forest fires occur naturally, they tend to move quickly through the forest. They burn the lower branches and clear the deadwood and weeds from the forest floor.

For many years, the federal government tried to prevent as many forest fires as possible. Forests built up layers of deadwood and brush. This left forests at risk for much fiercer natural fires. The extra deadwood served as fuel. It also kept forests less healthy for trees and wildlife.

Fires help to provide ideal growing conditions in forests. They also improve the forest as a habitat for large trees, such as Douglas firs and sequoias, that prefer some open space. These trees have large root systems that are not as efficient when they have to compete with other plants' root systems. In addition, forest fires help seeds to sprout. Some types of pinecones only release seeds when they are subjected to intense heat.

In recent years, forest-management techniques have changed. Scientists understand the importance of fire to the forest. Forest agencies have begun starting controlled fires. These help clear away the growth that has built up over so many years. At the same time, people have increased their use of the forest for leisure purposes. Now most forest fires are caused by human carelessness. People being careless with matches or cigarettes can start fires. Sometimes people leave their campfires unattended. These fires often cause more damage than natural fires because they upset the balance of nature. They also can destroy timber and harm the soil.

Always be careful when you are camping or walking through the woods. Be careful with matches and make sure campfires have been extinguished properly. We will all see the benefits from these precautions in our forests and natural environments.

Reading Time _____

Recalling Facts

1. Fires started by lightning are called
   - ❏ a. naturally occurring fires.
   - ❏ b. careless fires.
   - ❏ c. controlled fires.

2. _____, people began to believe that they needed to prevent forest fires.
   - ❏ a. Before 1900
   - ❏ b. After 1900
   - ❏ c. Before 1800

3. The process of preventing forest fires is called
   - ❏ a. fire incentives.
   - ❏ b. fire suppression.
   - ❏ c. fire involvement.

4. The burning process helps with the
   - ❏ a. quality of the air
   - ❏ b. migration of birds.
   - ❏ c. generation of new growth.

5. In recent years, forest agencies have begun starting
   - ❏ a. controlled fires.
   - ❏ b. natural fires.
   - ❏ c. random fires.

Understanding Ideas

6. You can assume that the longer deadwood and growth build up on the forest floor,
   - ❏ a. the more fierce a fire will be.
   - ❏ b. the less fierce a fire will be.
   - ❏ c. the less likely a fire will be.

7. If a forest fire moves rapidly through a forest, it is most likely
   - ❏ a. a helpful fire.
   - ❏ b. an extremely harmful fire.
   - ❏ c. a fire caused by carelessness with matches.

8. The best lesson one can learn about forest fires from this article is that
   - ❏ a. forest agencies work to control fires.
   - ❏ b. it is important to practice fire safety in the forest.
   - ❏ c. it is important to practice fire safety but only when the forest is dry.

9. As a result of fire suppression, people have learned
   - ❏ a. to identify new species of trees.
   - ❏ b. about climate changes.
   - ❏ c. how important fires are to the forest.

10. You can assume that a naturally occurring forest fire
    - ❏ a. destroys rather than benefits the forest.
    - ❏ b. will not damage property.
    - ❏ c. will be a benefit to many species

The Michigan sun was shining brightly this morning. "I've never seen a bird like that before," Susan said to her teacher, Ms. Sutter.

Ms. Sutter smiled. "A Kirtland's warbler! I'm glad you could see one!"

"Is it a rare bird?"

"It's an endangered species," Ms. Sutter said. "There are only about a thousand of them left. It's hard for these birds to survive because the only place they nest is here in the jack pines."

"Why is it hard for them to survive here?" Susan said.

"What's difficult about it is that only jack pines that are 7 to 15 years old have blueberries growing underneath them, and blueberries are the birds' favorite food. To grow new jack pines, their seeds must be spread. But the trees' pinecones only release seeds when there is a forest fire. When there are no fires, no seeds grow and there are no blueberries for the birds to eat."

"Why wouldn't there be any fires?" Susan asked.

"When there's too much rain and snow, the forest floor is too damp for naturally occurring fires. Foresters have helped the warblers by using controlled fires to help new trees sprout. People are trying to help the Kirtland's warbler thrive again. It will take time, though."

1. Recognizing Words in Context

Find the word *thrive* in the passage. One definition below is closest to the meaning of that word. One definition has the opposite or nearly opposite meaning. The remaining definition has a completely different meaning. Label the definitions C for *closest,* O for *opposite or nearly opposite,* and D for *different.*

_____ a. decrease in hunger

_____ b. increase in number

_____ c. decrease in number

2. Distinguishing Fact from Opinion

Two of the statements below present *facts,* which can be proved correct. The other statement is an *opinion,* which expresses someone's thoughts or beliefs. Label the statements F for *fact* and O for *opinion.*

_____ a. Kirtland's warbler is an endangered species.

_____ b. Forest fires help provide the habitat the Kirtland's warbler needs.

_____ c. All Kirtland's warblers should be placed in zoos that have young jack pines.

3. Keeping Events in Order

Label the statements below 1, 2, and 3 to show the order in which the events happened.

_____ a. Blueberry bushes grew.

_____ b. New jack pines sprouted.

_____ c. Foresters started controlled fires.

4. Making Correct Inferences

Two of the statements below are correct *inferences,* or reasonable guesses. They are based on information in the passage. The other statement is an incorrect, or faulty, inference. Label the statements C for *correct* inference and F for *faulty* inference.

_____ a. Kirtland's warblers feed on blueberries that grow among the jack pines.

_____ b. Fires should be allowed to burn wherever they occur.

_____ c. Kirtland's warblers may die out if their habitat cannot be preserved.

5. Understanding Main Ideas

One of the statements below expresses the main idea of the passage. One statement is too general, or too broad. The other explains only part of the passage; it is too narrow. Label the statements M for *main idea,* B for *too broad,* and N for *too narrow.*

_____ a. Endangered species must be protected.

_____ b. The Kirtland's warbler is rare because it requires a special habitat.

_____ c. There are only about 1,000 Kirtland's warblers left.

Correct Answers, Part A _____

Correct Answers, Part B _____

Total Correct Answers _____

The Sun was once our only source of light. Learning how to control light has made it easier for humans to survive.

Learning to control fire was a key discovery among early humans. Fire provides both light and heat. As early as 400,000 B.C., fire was kept in caves. The flaming torch was the first portable lamp. It gave humans a small bit of freedom from the dark. By 13,000 B.C., humans were making lamps from rocks, shells, and animal horns. These lamps were filled with animal or vegetable fat and used a fiber wick. By 500 B.C., pottery lamps were commonly used.

Candles first appeared in about A.D. 400. The best candles of the time were made of beeswax. They were used mainly in religious ceremonies. Candles weren't common in homes until the A.D.1300s.

Gas lighting appeared in 1792. William Murdock, known as the father of gas lighting, heated coal to make gas. He used that gas to heat and light his home. By 1823, nearly 40,000 coal-gas lamps lit 345 kilometers (215 miles) of streets in London. The 1850s brought the widespread use of kerosene as a fuel for lighting.

Thomas Edison created the first successful electric lamp in 1879. This lamp worked by using a carbonized thread as a filament. The filament was put into a glass bulb with all the air removed. Then Edison sent an electric current through the filament. This first attempt burned for 45 hours. It was the forerunner of our current electric lamps.

Edison's greatest contribution to the development of electric light was in filament design. He had tried many different types of filaments—wood, cardboard, glass, hair, and bamboo. In 1880, he was given a patent for his invention, which was called the incandescent lamp. By 1883, there were more than 300 electric-power stations in the United States. These supplied power to more than 70,000 incandescent lamps.

In 1937, the fluorescent lamp was shown at the New York World's Fair. These lamps have twice the efficiency and life of an incandescent lamp. Fluorescent bulbs traditionally had a long tube-shaped design. In the late 1980s, carbonized fluorescent light bulbs changed the industry. They are much more energy efficient than incandescent lamps and come in a variety of shapes.

The 21st century is sure to bring even more advances in how we light our homes. Researchers are always looking for ways to illuminate our lives.

Reading Time _____

Recalling Facts

1. Our first source of light was
   - ❏ a. fire.
   - ❏ b. a candle.
   - ❏ c. the Sun.

2. The first portable lamp was the
   - ❏ a. flaming torch.
   - ❏ b. flashlight.
   - ❏ c. candle.

3. Among the materials used to make prehistoric lamps were
   - ❏ a. pieces of cardboard.
   - ❏ b. shells.
   - ❏ c. steel.

4. Prehistoric lamps were fueled by
   - ❏ a. gasoline.
   - ❏ b. kerosene.
   - ❏ c. animal or vegetable fat.

5. At first, candles were used mainly in
   - ❏ a. schools.
   - ❏ b. religious ceremonies.
   - ❏ c. kitchens.

Understanding Ideas

6. Which of the following was probably not a major reason for humans' early interest in light?
   - ❏ a. fashion and design
   - ❏ b. safety and protection
   - ❏ c. ability to see in the dark

7. Since the time that early humans discovered how to create light, people have always tried to
   - ❏ a. find ways to reduce their needs for lamps.
   - ❏ b. discover ways to replace lamps.
   - ❏ c. improve the efficiency of lamps.

8. Which of the following statements is not true?
   - ❏ a. The electric lamp was the first development in lighting since the candle.
   - ❏ b. Gas for lighting can be made by burning coal.
   - ❏ c. Fluorescent lamps are much more efficient than incandescent lamps.

9. According to the passage, which of the following was Edison's greatest contribution to the electric lamp?
   - ❏ a. the glass bulb
   - ❏ b. the socket design
   - ❏ c. the filament design

10. In the future, advances in lighting will likely
    - ❏ a. decrease.
    - ❏ b. increase.
    - ❏ c. stay the same.

You Can Help Conserve Electricity

"Turn the lights off! Close the refrigerator door!"

Have your parents ever said those things to you? That's because they understand the importance of conserving electrical energy. Think of how much our world has changed in the past century. Living in homes lit by electricity is a relatively new situation compared with how long humans have lived on Earth.

Most electrical energy comes from power plants that burn fossil fuels, which include coal, petroleum, and natural gas. Fossil fuels take millions of years to form. They are a finite resource. That means that the fuels have limited supplies. It is up to us as consumers to preserve this valuable resource.

There are many simple ways you can help conserve right in your own home or school. An easy way is to make signs that say "Turn off the lights" and to place the signs above the light switches in your house. Another thing you can do is to put on a sweater, rather than turning up the heat, if you're cold. You can also purchase light bulbs that use less electricity than regular bulbs. You can replace all the light bulbs in your house with energy-efficient ones. Of course, the simplest thing you can do is to turn off lights and appliances when you aren't using them. You can make a difference for all of us!

1. **Recognizing Words in Context**

   Find the word *finite* in the passage. One definition below is closest to the meaning of that word. One definition has the opposite or nearly opposite meaning. The remaining definition has a completely different meaning. Label the definitions C for *closest*, O for *opposite or nearly opposite*, and D for *different*.

   _____ a. invented

   _____ b. limited

   _____ c. endless

2. **Distinguishing Fact from Opinion**

   Two of the statements below present *facts*, which can be proved correct. The other statement is an *opinion*, which expresses someone's thoughts or beliefs. Label the statements F for *fact* and O for *opinion*.

   _____ a. We need to do a better job of conserving electricity.

   _____ b. Fossil fuels are a finite resource.

   _____ c. Some light bulbs use less electricity than others do.

3. Keeping Events in Order

Label the statements below 1, 2, and 3 to show the order in which the events happen.

_____ a. Electricity flows into your house.

_____ b. Burning fossil fuels creates electricity.

_____ c. Fossil fuels begin forming.

4. Making Correct Inferences

Two of the statements below are correct *inferences*, or reasonable guesses. They are based on information in the passage. The other statement is an incorrect, or faulty, inference. Label the statements C for *correct* inference and F for *faulty* inference.

_____ a. It is important that we use electricity wisely.

_____ b. One person can't make a difference in conserving electricity.

_____ c. One day there may not be enough fossil fuels to meet our needs.

5. Understanding Main Ideas

One of the statements below expresses the main idea of the passage. One statement is too general, or too broad. The other explains only part of the passage; it is too narrow. Label the statements M for *main idea*, B for *too broad*, and N for *too narrow*.

_____ a. We use electricity in many ways.

_____ b. Conserving energy will help ensure there is enough electricity for everyone.

_____ c. You can help conserve energy by turning off lights.

Correct Answers, Part A _____

Correct Answers, Part B _____

Total Correct Answers _____

What Is the Wind?

Wind is a weather phenomenon found around us almost all the time. Wind is simply the movement of air from one place to another. Usually air will move from a place of high pressure to a place of low pressure. When it does, there is wind.

The atmosphere is made up mainly of nitrogen and oxygen gases that are held close to Earth by gravity. This gravitational pull creates air pressure. The air always presses down on us, even though you may think it is weightless. The entire atmosphere weighs more than five quadrillion tons! As you sit in your chair, the air is pressing on your body with 6.7 kilograms (14.7 pounds) of force.

Air pressure varies because temperature varies. Air is made up of gas molecules. When air warms, it expands. The molecules move farther apart, and the air pressure decreases. This is called low pressure. When air cools, it contracts. The molecules move closer together, and the air pressure increases. This is called high pressure.

Understanding how sea breezes form can help explain the mystery of wind. The breezes that occur along beaches are usually caused by the difference between the air pressure above the ocean and the air pressure above the land. Although the sun shines upon the ocean and the land simultaneously, the land warms up more quickly than the ocean does. This is because the warmer water on the surface of the ocean is continuously mixing with the cooler water from the deeper parts of the ocean.

On land, the air directly above the ground gets warmer, so it expands, creating lower pressure. As the air expands, it pushes upward. As the air rises, the air molecules begin to crowd closer together. This creates high pressure over the land. This hot air over the land moves out to the sea, where the pressure is lower. There, the air bunches up over the water so the air pressure over the water increases. The air near the ocean's surface flows back to the low pressure that is over the land, creating a gentle sea breeze.

High winds can develop when two masses of air with very different pressures come together. Weather forecasters can use their knowledge of air pressure, along with scientific instruments, to predict when there is a danger of high wind. Nature is tricky, however, so the forecasters are not always right.

Reading Time _____

Recalling Facts

1. Air usually moves from an area of
   - ❑ a. low pressure to high pressure.
   - ❑ b. high pressure to low pressure.
   - ❑ c. low pressure to low pressure.

2. Air pressure varies because
   - ❑ a. temperature changes.
   - ❑ b. weather occurs.
   - ❑ c. clouds form.

3. A low-pressure area consists of air molecules that are
   - ❑ a. a normal distance from each other.
   - ❑ b. farther apart than normal.
   - ❑ c. closer together than normal.

4. Warm air tends to
   - ❑ a. move downward.
   - ❑ b. stay in the same place.
   - ❑ c. move upward.

5. What creates air pressure?
   - ❑ a. the pull of gravity on air
   - ❑ b. the movement of ocean tides
   - ❑ c. changes in wind speed

Understanding Ideas

6. The warmest air in a room would most likely be found near
   - ❑ a. the floor.
   - ❑ b. the ceiling.
   - ❑ c. a window.

7. If you are at the ocean and feel a sea breeze, you can assume that
   - ❑ a. there is low pressure over the land.
   - ❑ b. high-pressure air from the sea is moving over the land.
   - ❑ c. the pressure over the land and sea are equal.

8. If a mass of warm air moves into an area that has much cooler air, you can expect
   - ❑ a. strong winds.
   - ❑ b. gentle breezes.
   - ❑ c. fog.

9. You could conclude from the article that the
   - ❑ a. wind's patterns are random.
   - ❑ b. wind almost always occurs as a storm.
   - ❑ c. wind occurs in many ways.

10. The air over the ocean doesn't warm as quickly as the air over the land because
    - ❑ a. surface water mixes with deeper water.
    - ❑ b. the Sun is closer to the land than the sea.
    - ❑ c. the ocean reflects sunlight.

Making a Wind Vane

A wind vane, also called a weather vane, is one of the oldest tools for measuring wind direction. Knowing the wind direction can help people predict storms and weather patterns.

You can make your own wind vane by gathering together the following materials: scissors, cardboard, a compass, a plastic soft drink bottle, a plastic drinking straw, a felt marking pen, and a shallow pan filled with rocks.

Cut an arrow from the piece of cardboard. Include a small tab halfway between the arrow end and the tail end. Make sure the tail end is wider than the arrow end. Bend the tab slightly and insert the tab into the top of the drinking straw. The arrow should turn easily. Put the other end of the straw in the soft drink bottle. Then remove enough rocks from the pan so you can place the bottle in it. Pile the rocks back around the bottle so the bottle won't blow over. Next, use the felt-tip pen to mark the directions north, south, east, and west on the bottle.

Set the wind vane securely on top of something high enough to catch the wind—for example, a playground slide. Check your directions with the compass to make sure the word *north* is facing north. Record the wind direction daily to see whether there is a connection between the wind direction and the weather.

1. Recognizing Words in Context

Find the word *securely* in the passage. One definition below is closest to the meaning of that word. One definition has the opposite or nearly opposite meaning. The remaining definition has a completely different meaning. Label the definitions C for *closest*, O for *opposite or nearly opposite*, and D for *different*.

_____ a. expertly

_____ b. firmly

_____ c. loosely

2. Distinguishing Fact from Opinion

Two of the statements below present *facts*, which can be proved correct. The other statement is an *opinion*, which expresses someone's thoughts or beliefs. Label the statements F for *fact* and O for *opinion*.

_____ a. A wind vane is one of the oldest tools for predicting weather.

_____ b. Wind vanes are one of the best devices for predicting approaching storms.

_____ c. A compass is used to find directions.

3. Keeping Events in Order

Label the statements below 1, 2, and 3 to show the order in which the events happen.

_____ a. The wind vane is placed on top of something high.

_____ b. The wind catches the wind vane and makes it point in a certain direction.

_____ c. Materials are assembled to construct a wind vane.

4. Making Correct Inferences

Two of the statements below are correct *inferences,* or reasonable guesses. They are based on information in the passage. The other statement is an incorrect, or faulty, inference. Label the statements C for *correct* inference and F for *faulty* inference.

_____ a. Recording wind directions can help you predict storms.

_____ b. A wind vane is a simple tool to construct.

_____ c. Your weather predictions from the wind vane will always be correct.

5. Understanding Main Ideas

One of the statements below expresses the main idea of the passage. One statement is too general, or too broad. The other explains only part of the passage; it is too narrow. Label the statements M for *main idea,* B for *too broad,* and N for *too narrow.*

_____ a. Wind direction can be measured in several ways.

_____ b. Cardboard is used to make the arrow for the wind vane.

_____ c. A wind vane can be made from items that are easy to get.

Correct Answers, Part A _____

Correct Answers, Part B _____

Total Correct Answers _____

ANSWER KEY

READING RATE GRAPH

COMPREHENSION SCORE GRAPH

COMPREHENSION SKILLS PROFILE GRAPH

Answer Key

1A	1. c	2. a	3. b	4. c	5. c	6. b	7. a	8. b	9. a	10. b
1B	1. C, D, O	2. F, F, O	3. 2, 3, 1	4. C, C, F	5. N, M, B
2A	1. a	2. a	3. b	4. a	5. c	6. b	7. a	8. c	9. b	10. b
2B	1. O, C, D	2. F, F, O	3. 2, 1, 3	4. C, C, F	5. M, N, B
3A	1. b	2. a	3. c	4. c	5. a	6. b	7. a	8. a	9. c	10. b
3B	1. C, O, D	2. F, F, O	3. 2, 1, 3	4. C, F, C	5. M, N, B
4A	1. b	2. c	3. c	4. b	5. a	6. c	7. c	8. a	9. b	10. a
4B	1. C, D, O	2. O, F, F	3. 1, 3, 2	4. C, F, C	5. N, B, M
5A	1. b	2. a	3. c	4. a	5. b	6. c	7. a	8. b	9. b	10. c
5B	1. C, D, O	2. F, O, F	3. 3, 2, 1	4. C, F, C	5. B, N, M
6A	1. b	2. c	3. a	4. b	5. c	6. b	7. b	8. c	9. a	10. a
6B	1. D, C, O	2. O, F, F	3. 1, 3, 2	4. C, F, C	5. N, B, M
7A	1. b	2. a	3. c	4. a	5. b	6. c	7. b	8. b	9. a	10. c
7B	1. O, C, D	2. O, F, F	3. 3, 2, 1	4. F, C, C	5. B, M, N
8A	1. b	2. c	3. b	4. c	5. a	6. c	7. b	8. a	9. a	10. c
8B	1. O, C, D	2. F, O, F	3. 1, 3, 2	4. C, C, F	5. M, N, B
9A	1. a	2. b	3. a	4. c	5. a	6. b	7. a	8. a	9. a	10. a
9B	1. D, O, C	2. F, F, O	3. 1, 2, 3	4. C, F, C	5. M, B, N
10A	1. c	2. a	3. b	4. a	5. c	6. c	7. a	8. b	9. b	10. a
10B	1. D, O, C	2. O, F, F	3. 2, 3, 1	4. C, F, C	5. N, B, M
11A	1. c	2. b	3. a	4. c	5. b	6. a	7. c	8. a	9. b	10. b
11B	1. D, O, C	2. F, O, F	3. 2, 1, 3	4. F, C, C	5. B, N, M
12A	1. a	2. b	3. b	4. c	5. c	6. c	7. a	8. c	9. b	10. c
12B	1. C, O, D	2. O, F, F	3. 3, 2, 1	4. C, C, F	5. M, N, B
13A	1. a	2. c	3. b	4. a	5. c	6. a	7. c	8. a	9. c	10. b
13B	1. O, D, C	2. O, F, F	3. 1, 3, 2	4. C, F, C	5. B, M, N

14A	1. c	2. b	3. a	4. b	5. c	6. c	7. c	8. c	9. b	10. a
14B	1. D, O, C	2. O, F, F	3. 1, 3, 2	4. C, F, C	5. N, B, M
15A	1. a	2. b	3. c	4. b	5. c	6. a	7. b	8. b	9. a	10. b
15B	1. C, O, D	2. F, F, O	3. 2, 3, 1	4. C, F, C	5. B, M, N
16A	1. b	2. a	3. c	4. a	5. b	6. b	7. a	8. c	9. b	10. a
16B	1. D, O, C	2. F, F, O	3. 2, 3, 1	4. F, C, C	5. B, M, N
17A	1. a	2. b	3. c	4. b	5. a	6. b	7. a	8. a	9. c	10. a
17B	1. D, O, C	2. F, O, F	3. 1, 3, 2	4. C, C, F	5. N, M, B
18A	1. c	2. b	3. b	4. c	5. a	6. b	7. a	8. a	9. c	10. c
18B	1. C, O, D	2. F, F, O	3. 3, 2, 1	4. C, C, F	5. M, N, B
19A	1. a	2. c	3. b	4. a	5. b	6. b	7. c	8. c	9. b	10. a
19B	1. C, O, D	2. F, O, F	3. 2, 3, 1	4. C, C, F	5. M, B, N
20A	1. a	2. a	3. c	4. b	5. c	6. b	7. a	8. a	9. a	10. c
20B	1. O, D, C	2. F, O, F	3. 2, 1, 3	4. F, C, C	5. N, B, M
21A	1. b	2. a	3. a	4. c	5. a	6. c	7. c	8. a	9. b	10. a
21B	1. D, C, O	2. F, F, O	3. 3, 1, 2	4. C, F, C	5. B, N, M
22A	1. c	2. a	3. c	4. b	5. c	6. a	7. b	8. c	9. b	10. a
22B	1. C, O, D	2. O, F, F	3. 1, 2, 3	4. C, C, F	5. B, N, M
23A	1. a	2. b	3. b	4. c	5. a	6. a	7. a	8. b	9. c	10. c
23B	1. D, C, O	2. F, F, O	3. 3, 2, 1	4. C, F, C	5. B, M, N
24A	1. c	2. a	3. b	4. c	5. b	6. a	7. c	8. a	9. c	10. b
24B	1. D, O, C	2. O, F, F	3. 3, 2, 1	4. C, F, C	5. B, M, N
25A	1. b	2. a	3. b	4. c	5. a	6. b	7. b	8. a	9. c	10. a
25B	1. D, C, O	2. F, O, F	3. 2, 3, 1	4. C, C, F	5. B, N, M

READING RATE

Put an X on the line above each lesson number to show your reading time and words-per-minute rate for that lesson.

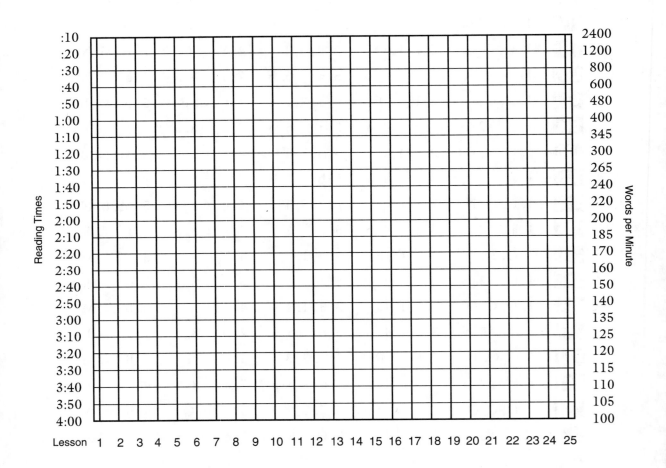